I0412705

THEIR OWN VOICES:
ORAL ACCOUNTS
OF EARLY SETTLERS IN
WASHINGTON COUNTY, NEW YORK

Collected by
DR. ASA FITCH
1847–1878

Edited by
WINSTON ADLER

Edited portions from an original manuscript owned by
**THE NEW YORK GENEALOGICAL
AND BIOGRAPHICAL SOCIETY**
155 EAST 58TH STREET
NEW YORK, NY 10022-1939

©*Copyright 1983*
by Winston Adler

ISBN: 1-4636-4892-8
ISBN-13: 9781463648923
Printed in the United States of America

TABLE OF CONTENTS

PREFACE

Dr. Asa Fitch (1809-1879) of Salem, New York, was a
medical doctor and naturalist who also had a great interest in
the history of his native Washington County. In 1847 Dr. Fitch
began work on what was to become a life-long oral history
project in the county. He visited elderly friends and neighbors and questioned them about "early times"—the days of
first settlement, the Revolutionary War, and the thirty years
or so following the war. He carefully wrote out their statements and preserved these, together with other papers, in a
large manuscript, "Notes for a History of Washington County."
The original of this manuscript is now in the collection of the
New York Genealogical and Biographical Society in New York
City; a microfilm copy is kept in the Washington County Clerk's
Office in Fort Edward, New York.

Dr. Fitch collected many of his statements in 1847 and
1848, when he was preparing a short history and geography
of the county for the New York State Agricultural Society.
His "History and Topography of Washington County" was
published by the Society in its *Transactions and Proceedings
for 1848-49*. Dr. Fitch drew on some of the oral accounts to
write the history part of this work, but he made use of only
a small fraction of all the material he had by then copied and
compiled (several hundred manuscript pages at least). There
are probably five hundred or more pages of oral accounts in
the whole of the "Notes," mixed in with other information
Dr. Fitch gathered from gravestones, deeds, diaries, town
records and some published histories having to do with the
county's past.

In 1979, thanks to the encouragement of Sandra Mc-
Clellan of the Greenwich Journal–Salem Press, I began to copy
short passages from Dr. Fitch's oral records and submit them
to the newspaper. I skipped about in the manuscript (it is
over eighteen hundred pages), choosing the stories and statements I liked and then sometimes editing them—cutting out

dull parts and also anything that sounded like poor second or third-hand information. When I had collected a large pile of newspaper clippings, I started to think of putting them together into a book. This collection, *Their Own Voices: Oral Accounts of Early Settlers in Washington County, New York*, consists of the newspaper pieces that appeared in the Journal–Press between August 1979 and June 1981, plus some passages not published before. The short statements have been arranged in rough chronological order to make an oral history of the county from the beginning of settlement in the 1760's through the first decades of the nineteenth century.

It is an incomplete history, of course, but full of fascinating details and incidents. The voices of the "speakers" are simple and believable. Though some people were remembering back seventy years or more, I think we can feel confident no one was inventing or embroidering anything. In most cases, Dr. Fitch has preserved the actual words of the people he spoke with. He didn't have a tape recorder (naturally) but he probably used some form of shorthand at the time of his interviews. Later, when he copied the statements in longhand into his manuscript, he sometimes edited them or added words of his own. He states this clearly on occasion. But this appears to have been the exception rather than the rule.

I hope most readers won't mind the fact that a modern editor has cut a little here and there. But for those who want to see the unabridged version, each statement has a note giving its numbered location in the manuscript. (Dr. Fitch's manuscript has no index or page numbers, only "note numbers.") No words have been added to the original text without the use of editor's brackets. There is one small exception: in the few cases where an account begins as a story told in the third person and then switches to the first person, pronouns have been made to agree with the body of the account. For the most part, I have not footnoted the short introductions to the statements; that seemed too much like putting footnotes on footnotes. The facts there come mainly from the Fitch manuscript itself (from portions of the statements which haven't reached print) or from Crisfield Johnson's 1878 *History of Washington County*.

I would like to thank Sally Brillon, former Director of Historic Preservation in Washington County, and Leon Putnam, County Clerk, for their original help with this project, without which it would have been quite impossible. My thanks also go to the New York Genealogical and Biographical Society for permission to publish from the Fitch manuscript, and to the Washington County Historical Society for their interest and encouragement.

W. A.

PART ONE:

COMING ONTO THE LAND

THE SETTLERS

In these accounts we hear the stories of families who settled in the five present-day towns of Salem, Jackson, Argyle, Greenwich, and Hebron. Dr. Fitch definitely interviewed more of his near neighbors in and around Salem than people in the towns farther from his home. But it is also true that the southern part of the county—particularly the Salem-Argyle area—was settled earlier than most of the north. And some important early settlements like Kingsbury and Skenesborough (now Whitehall) were almost totally broken up during the Revolutionary War, since they were Tory strongholds. Thus few of their original settlers or their children were around in the 1840's or 1850's to talk with Dr. Fitch.

William McCollister was a younger son of Hamilton McCollister, one of the first settlers and original proprietors of the town of Salem (first called White Creek). Hamilton and his companions were second and third-generation Scotch-Irish whose families had settled in western Massachusetts in the 1730's and 1740's. In 1764, they (and others) obtained a patent, "The Turner Patent," for 25,000 acres lying in the present town of Salem. A year later, the Massachusetts men deeded one-half of the Salem land to two New York gentlemen— probably the public officials who had helped get the charter from the provincial government. The two gentlemen immediately leased their portion to Dr. Thomas Clark and his congregation of new immigrants from County Monaghan, Ireland. These Scotch-Irish families moved onto their leaseholds between 1765 and 1770. Hamilton McCollister and the other men from Massachusetts founded the "New England" Colony in the town which kept a little apart from Dr. Clark's congregation for some time.

William McCollister:

Father Hamilton McCollister came to Salem when a young man in company with James Turner and Joshua Conkey, who had wives but left them at home. They came from Pelham in Massachusetts and were here two or three years before the town was chartered, coming onto the land as squatters. They first put up a hut on the same spot where the Coffee House now stands in the village of Salem. Flat, level land was the only kind that was much esteemed in those days. We still have Father's old musket which he brought with him at this time and which is marked with his initials and the date Seventeen Hundred and Fifty-six—one of the best guns in the country.

The three men kept bachelor's hall together the first year or two, probably going back to Pelham in the winter. Immediately after erecting their cabin in the woods they commenced clearing up a strip of land each for himself: Turner cutting the timber off the piece in the meadow north of the Academy, Father making a clearing around where Alexander Wright's house now stands, and Conkey going further up the creek. Each of them put up a small log house on his clearing and by the second year, I think, each was living by himself in his own cabin.

Father too lived for awhile in Stillwater. [*Once*] on returning to his house here from Stillwater, he found a large catamount lying dead on the floor. The door was made of soft and perhaps green basswood which he had split into rude boards and pegged or nailed together—the substitute to which they then resorted for want of sawed boards. The catamount had gnawed a hole through this door and come in and got at some unguentum which was laying on one of the crossbeams overhead—the remedy for itch which in those days was an indispensable article in every dwelling—and had ate and licked the ointment nearly clean from off the beam. This he always supposed had poisoned the animal so that she died on the spot, for he knew not how otherwise to account for her death.

He pulled her out of the door and washed up the floor around where she laid. In the evening, it being a dark night,

he was startled at observing at the hole in the door two balls of light like two candles which he well knew were the eyes of another catamount peering in upon him. He grasped his gun but the motion alarmed the animal and the lights disappeared. He now placed his gun at a rest, aiming directly at the hole in the door, and awaited the reappearance of the lights. They soon returned, and cautiously taking a more deliberate aim, he fired. The gun was reloaded with all convenient dispatch, but the lights appeared no more. He now barricaded the hole in the door and laid himself down to sleep. On opening the door next morning, there lay dead a large catamount which was evidently the mate of the one he had found dead in the house.

At the close of the first or second year after Father came here, he returned to Pelham and married his wife and brought her up with him the following season. I think she was here one summer before either Turner or Conkey moved their families up. At Stillwater was the nearest gristmill, when Mother first came here, and she used to relate that on one occasion when Father had gone down there—about thirty miles as they then used to go—on horseback, to get a grist ground, a bear came boldly up to the door of the house and grasped and carried off their sow from the midst of her litter of pigs, and she had no means of preventing the depredation.[1]

Tryphena Martin Angel was born in Salem in 1775. Her father, Moses Martin—like a number of others—had come to the town as an independent settler. The "Yankee" Moses Martin was one of the leaders of the New England community and served as an early Justice of the Peace.

Tryphena Martin Angel:

I once asked Uncle Adam Martin whether our family was English, Scotch or Irish in its origin. He said it was neither—that his great-grandfather emigrated from Wales to America. This is all that is known of our origin.

My grandmother's maiden name was Newell of Sturbridge. By her first husband Martin she had in addition to the three sons, Adam, Aaron, and Moses the following daughters, I think: Elizabeth, Sarah, Tryphena. After the death of her first husband, who died when Father was but three or four years old, grandmother married an Ellis by whom she had Reuben, Amasa, and Moses. They lived in Shaftsbury, Vermont, where she died. She was a very religious woman. The Martin children disliked her calling one of her Ellis children Moses, as she already had a son by that name. But she said she loved the name—that she named all her children out of the Bible and thought Moses was one of the prettiest names she could find there.

My father, Moses Martin, being but a few years old when his father died and his mother married a second husband, was brought up by an uncle of his in Sturbridge. He was in service in the Old French War and on its close, being still a young man, came to Stillwater where he taught school and where he married. My mother's father was Ephraim More. He came from Simsbury, Connecticut, to Stillwater. He worked in the Simsbury mines and by an explosion in the mines his eyes were so burnt that he became partially and ere long entirely blind.

[Father] *was located on a farm on the east side of the river for a while and his two eldest children, I think, Aaron and Miriam, were born here.*

It took Father two days to come here from Stillwater. He came with his goods in an ox cart and had to stop and cut the road in places. Livingston, Roger Reid, Esquire McNaughton and I think William Reid here on the Point were all here before him.[2]

The McNeil family were part of still another group of Scotch-Irish who came to this country in 1738–40 under the leadership of a Colonel Laughlin Campbell. This group had failed to get a grant of land when they first arrived, and had been living among the Dutch along the Hudson and in the "Highlands" [Ulster County] for a generation. In 1764 they received over 47,000 acres, "The Argyle Patent," in present-day Argyle, Greenwich and Fort Edward.

William McNeil's Father:

My grandfather Archibald McNeil drew Lot Number Eleven of the Argyle Patent. With my father, John McNeil, he came up here in Seventeen Hundred and Sixty-eight and cleared some land and got in a crop of wheat. They brought flour with them and got their bread baked at Duncan Campbell's on Duelly's Hill, and for meat depended on game. The long gun, taller than I am, is still preserved in the family, and with this Father could take off a partridge's head—for it injured it for eating to be shot through the body. They returned to the Highlands, and came up again the following year and laid up the logs for a house.

In May Seventeen Hundred and Seventy they arrived in Argyle with the family. The house was twenty feet by twenty-four, made of flattened logs, but as yet without a roof, window or door. Some boards had been drawed to the house in the winter by sleigh from Schuylerville, pursuant to an agreement made there with a man the fall before. These boards were set up endwise, leaning against the house to form a shed under which they slept till the house was roofed.

A door and windows were sawed in the logs with a cross-cut saw. Shingles of pine, three foot long and three-quarters of an inch thick at the butt, were got out and nailed with wrought nails to slats split out of oak and fastened to the raf-

7

ters a foot apart. The shingles were laid one foot to the weather, and stayed on till Eighteen Hundred and Twenty-two. The part exposed to the weather was then mostly worn away, but the remaining part was perfectly sound. In sawing the door and windows, a log being sawed off and removed, a pinhole was bored diagonally into the ends thus exposed and down into the log below, and a pin drove in on each side of the door. Then a section of the next log was sawed off and removed and the ends thus exposed were similarly pinned.

Neal Gillespie's family came up to Argyle at the same time in company with Grandfather's. There were no families in that part of Argyle then. Perhaps Yerry Killmore was at the Corners.[3]

Susan Lyttle Vance was the fifth child of John Lyttle and his wife, who were members of Dr. Clark's congregation. Clark and his followers left Ireland in April 1764. By 1765 they were living in Stillwater, where they "occupied the open ground in and around [the] *fort, and the soldiers, whenever any butchering was done for their own supply, would give a portion of the meat to Dr. Clark's company—several of the families were so destitute . . ."*[4] *These facts may help us to read between the lines of the brief statement below.*

Susan Lyttle Vance:

I was born at Schuylerville in the barracks there in sight of General Schuyler's residence, April Seventh, Seventeen Hundred and Sixty-seven, and when four years old was brought to Salem. My father had previously been out to Salem and put up a little cabin. Although it was full of cracks and without a chimney or floor and only a flat stone leaning against one side of the enclosure—against which stone a fire could be built—on entering the cabin Mother with her babe in her arms danced around and around it, so overjoyed was she to set her foot in a house she could call her own.[5]

8

William and Caty Campbell, the son and daughter of "Black" Duncan Campbell, tell his story. Campbell must have been a poor man. Neither a proprietor nor a tenant, he came onto the land as a squatter and the "hanger-on" of a richer settler, "White" or "Old" Duncan Campbell. "White" Duncan Campbell was one of the proprietors of a special ten thousand–acre patent issued one year before the Argyle Patent to the actual blood descendants of Laughlin Campbell. "White" Duncan's lot lies in the present-day town of Greenwich.

William Campbell:

My father, Duncan Campbell, was born at Craignish or some such-named place in Argyleshire, I think.

Caty Campbell:

When he was fourteen years old he went to visit some relations of his in Ireland. With two other boys and three girls, amusing themselves on the seashore, they saw a ship hoisting her sails—as they understood, to make a short cruise around in the harbor—and thinking it would be a pleasant excursion they got on board of her. But she stood directly out to sea, and night coming on they lost sight of their native

land forever—crying bitterly but their tears of no avail. The captain brought them to Maryland where he got places for them, binding them out for four years. At parting the captain gave my father his blessing and best hopes, charging the man to whom he was bound to be kind to him, which he was, at the end of the four years allowing him to make a great party to which all his friends were invited. [*Despite the 'kindness' of the captain and Duncan's master, it is clear that Duncan and his companions were tricked into boarding the ship and*

9

later sold at so much per head in Maryland. At this period, ship captains received about five pounds apiece for every bond-servant delivered to the colonies.]

Hearing that labor was scarce and help greatly needed in harvest-time in the Highlands above New York, Father came there and there got acquainted with the other Duncan Campbell [*"White" Duncan*], to whom he attached himself. And for fifty years he lived neighbor to him and his son Archy with perfect friendship and confidence in each other. There was never the scratch of a pen between them in their business transactions in all that time.

William Campbell:

He came to the Highlands in this state, and when there enlisted as one of the New York troops in the Old French War under Colonel James Clinton and was stationed off on the western frontier as far as Detroit at one time. His company went down Lake Ontario and the Saint Lawrence with all the other troops from that direction, forming one of the three divisions that met at Montreal and forced it to surrender.

My father went thence back to the Highlands and soon after came here, having charge of Lot Fifty of the Scots Patent which belonged to somebody of the name of McKissam, I think—on which lot he settled and built a log house four or five rods from the kill which in high weather used to be up all around our house. [*This lot directly adjoined the land of "White" Duncan Campbell.*] His wife Mary Chambers from Ireland was one of the company that came over with Doctor Clark. None of her relations, I believe, came over with her.

My father never had any title to the land, but I and my brother afterwards bought it. It was all pine timber on the flat there adjoining the hill. On the level between my present house and the kill was chiefly pine mixed with some large oaks, birch, et cetera. There and north of here the hemlock predominated.[6]

Eunice Campbell Reid's father, William Campbell, was an-
other poor ex-soldier like "Black" Duncan Campbell. He also
lived as a dependant of "White" Duncan for some time. Was
there a clan tie which drew these men of the same name to-
gether?

Eunice Campbell Reid:

My father, William Campbell, was born on the Isle of
Skye, Scotland, and at the solicitation of his uncle, Captain
Campbell, he enlisted into his company ere he was yet twenty-
one years old and came to America. Captain Campbell's company belonging to a regiment commanded by Colonel Mont-
gomery. They came to America in time of the Old French
War and were at Allegheny, Detroit, Lower Canada, et cetera, in a number of engagements.

My father served nine years in the army and was discharged in Nova Scotia. I think so from the circumstance that
he there got acquainted with and married my mother. She
was born in Scotland in Argyleshire. Her maiden name was
Catherine Kennedy and she had been married to a man named
Thompson and was left a widow with eleven children, my
half-brothers and sisters. I was born in Nova Scotia. My father
came thence to New York, and we lived out in New Jersey
awhile. Then he came up here and might have settled on
land of his own if he had applied for it—soldier's rights over
on the edge of Vermont on Indian River—but he thought it
was so entirely out of the world there that he would not go
there. So he settled on the corner of Duncan Campbell's lot
down the hill this side of Battenville. He cleared up the flat
immediately below the dug-way. Stayed there three years.

My mother died there and was buried in the Eequire
McNaughton burying ground. I was my father's only child by
her. My half-brothers and sisters got scattered about and none
of them are now remaining around here. Father then moved
to Salem near Sodom [*Shushan*], next north the Widow French
farm and immediately joining it. Here we stayed till the troubles and dangers of the Revolution induced [*the family*] to
leave there, and come and live at Roger Reid's. I lived with

11

Hugh More two or three years, working in his family till Seventeen Hundred and Seventy-seven. The troubles in the country became so great I came home to my father's at Roger Reid's.

[Reid] had but one son, named Duncan, and one daughter, Catherine, who was my father's second wife. She had one son, Roger Campbell, my half-brother. Roger Reid drew the lot on which he lived, and put up the house of square logs there. After the war Father bought the place of Roger Reid, where my half-brother now lives, and there died. He might have got a farm much cheaper once. He owned a large Narragans horse and landlord Dick of Cambridge offered him the Widow Gray farm just west of Salem Village for that horse. But Father declined the offer, not needing the farm himself, and buying land to speculate on was never thought of at that day.[7]

The Blake party emigrated independently, though they probably had some friend or relative in the area. Robert Blake's father leased land on the "Anaquassacook Patent"—granted in 1762 to a number of Schenectady men. His Uncle Bell either bought or leased a lot in a section of the Argyle Patent which is now part of Fort Edward.

Robert Blake:

I was born in Scotland on the borders of England on the banks of the Water Liddle. When ten years old, in Seventeen Hundred and Seventy-one, I came to this country with my father and my mother, my uncle William Bell and our neighbor George Telford also coming over in company with us.

We came to New York and thence up the Hudson. My mother had been sick all the way and died at Tappan Bay and was buried in a graveyard on the east shore of the bay. We came on—stopped a few days in Albany, living in the old fort up on the hill—then came up to Saratoga, now called Schuylerville. There was a large barrack on the north side of the mouth of Fish Creek, close on the bank, with a very deep

SCHUYLER'S MILLS, SARATOGA.

ditch on its west and north sides—the Hudson guarding it on the east and Fish Creek on the south. Over this ditch was a drawbridge. A Dutchman and his family lived in and kept this barrack. On the flat outside of the ditch were two other barracks—not very large buildings, but very well built with brick chimneys, which were seldom seen so far in the country at that time. These had all been built in the Old French War. General Schuyler's house and sawmills were also there; a man was keeping Schuyler's house, he being away. We emigrant families occupied one of the barracks during our stay there, and there Francis Telford died and was buried.

Thence we came over to this neighborhood, arriving here the last of August, I should think—harvesting was over with. We—Telford's family, my father and I—moved into an empty house which had been built by one Germond several years before, at Fitch's Point. Here we lived several weeks till we had contracted for the farm down the hill in Jackson where most of my life was passed. We moved down there in the fall of Seventeen Hundred and Seventy-one, in a very large canoe that was loaned us and which took all our furniture at one load directly from the Germond house to our future home.[8]

Donald McDonald and Isabel Duncan MacIntyre, the children of two of his tenants, tell the story of the Reverend Harry Munro, an ambitious gentleman settler. Munro was trying to

13

establish a European-style estate like that of "Lord" Skene further north, though on a smaller scale. There were many military patents in Washington County—grants to officers and soldiers after the French and Indian War. Most were never settled by their original proprietors.

Donald McDonald:

Reverend Harry Munro was a Highlander and an Episcopal clergyman. He was chaplain to a Highland regiment, thus ranking as lieutenant. He consequently on his discharge was entitled to two thousand acres of land. This he drew in Hebron [1764]. On being discharged he settled for some time in New Jersey. He there lost his first wife, a fine handsome woman, mother of his only daughter, Betsey.

Munro got acquainted with Norman McCloud I suppose in New Jersey, as McCloud was once living there on Lord Stirling's estate. He too was a Scotchman and a discharged soldier. John Duncan and Donald McCloud he probably found in Albany. One Estee and another family also came on: six families in all that settled first on his patent, Father being one of them.

Munro's house stood near the outlet of the marsh on the west side of the brook, some four or six rods from the brook and sixty or eighty rods north of the marsh. It was a log house covered with bark and had but a single room some sixteen feet by twenty. No bedroom or pantry. I think it had no floor— the earth trod down firm and hard and could be swept clean. The first thing Munro did was to ditch the marsh, which covers thirty-five acres. A main ditch was dug along the east side for the brook to run in that comes in at the head of the marsh, and side drains were dug emptying into this. This part of the marsh was so far reclaimed as to produce wild grass. Captain John Armstrong used to come up here and cut hay and draw it home to Salem for several years.

Munro used to assemble his settlers on the Sabbath and preach to them, but it was only occasionally. At such times they gathered by the side of his house and he used to stand with his back to the house and his face towards the meadows;

14

and they used to say that he seemed to be adoring his meadows more than his God. He doted on the meadows excessively as is well known.

Munro was only here part of the time, when they were engaged in ditching or some such work. I think he had a house which he occupied in Albany or else in Rye, for he was much of the time in these places.[9]

Isabel Duncan McIntyre:

Munro was a large, fine-looking man. He promised the folks, as an inducement to settle on his land, that he would preach for them when he had leisure—but I believe I never head him but once. He was not up to his word in this particular.[10]

Donald McDonald relates his own family history. Though it is not directly stated, Donald's father did not settle on his soldier's grant because of the "New Hampshire Grants" troubles. Land along the present Vermont-New York border was then hotly disputed between "the Bennington People," led by Ethan Allen, and those with New York grants. (Eunice Campbell Reid's father probably stayed off his land for the same reason.)

Donald McDonald:

My father, John McDonald, belonged to a regiment of Highland soldiers—the Seventy-seventh Regiment of Foot—and served in that regiment seven years in America in time of the Old French War. Each soldier discharged from the Seventy-seventh was entitled to a certain amount of land. A private drew fifty acres, a non-commissioned officer two hundred. Father was with the surveyors as an assistant when they were laying out the soldiers' rights in this country, and selected his land on Indian River. South of the southeast part of Byrne's patent is a tier of small lots. First are five lots of two hundred acres each, then one of fifty acres, then one of two hundred acres. This last was the one selected by Father. The lot was eighty-eight chains and seventy-nine links in length,

15

east and west, and twenty-three chains and sixty-seven links in breadth. Two thirds of Father's lot lay in the state of Vermont when the state line came to be settled.

Father returned to Scotland but did not get a deed of his two hundred acres to take home with him. He there married, and December Fifteenth, Seventeen Hundred and Sixty-eight, I was born in Invernesshire, Parish of Urqhart. When I was five years old Father emigrated to America with Mother, myself, and an uncle of mine, James, who was living at Johnstown and was one of Sir John Johnson's retainers who fled with him to Canada, enduring most appalling sufferings from cold and hunger on the way. James was not a Catholic, though many of Johnson's Scotch families may have been. After the Revolution, he came from Canada and lived and died with us in Hebron.

Three months after our arrival in America, Mother died at Normanskill near Albany, giving birth to a daughter, Christine. At Normanskill, so Uncle James used to often say, among the Dutch children I wholly lost my mother tongue, the Gaelic language, in the space of twenty days. The infant Christine was taken care of by some friends in Albany. I also lived two years in Albany with John McDonald who, though of the same name, was no connection of Father's.

Father went to Johnstown with the view of getting a farm of old Sir William Johnson and arrived there as the old baronet was dying of bilious colic. He therefore returned to Albany. I suppose he casually fell in with Harry Munro there, as Munro was looking up settlers to move onto his land. He then came up here and looked at Munro's land and at his own. Finding his own lot mostly in Vermont, all but sixty-two acres, he gave up the idea of settling on it. Father therefore leased a lot of Munro—one hundred acres. The lots were carelessly run out and vary in size from eighty to one hundred and twenty acres in each. His lot was the northeast one in Munro's Patent. He took a lease for twenty-one years and paid an annual rent of five pounds per year—one shilling per acre.

Father put up a small log house covering it with black ash bark, without any floor. It was about two miles northeast of the Meadows. Before we moved up, he in the space of two years cleared six or seven acres, and for these two years he had not his axe on a grindstone. His only way of sharpening it was to rub it on a large stone or boulder lying on the ground. The Scotch were not expert with the axe. One Yankee would outchop three Scotchmen.

The nearest mill was Reid's at Fitch's Point, Salem, fifteen or seventeen miles distant, and Father used to carry a bushel of wheat that distance on his back. The second year after we came here, Captain Fitch's mill at Algiers in Pawlet, Vermont, was completed. This was ten miles distant. The next mill erected was eight miles distant at Middle Granville—put up by one Spring, a seaman.

Before moving us up here, Father married Marjory Cummings, a Highland woman in Albany. She died when I was ten years old, leaving a daughter, Elizabeth. After her death, we grew up—myself, Christine and Elizabeth—in the woods, with no mother and no housekeeper to take care of us or prepare our food and clothes. [11]

Isabel Duncan McIntyre:

I was born in Scotland March Fifteenth, Seventeen Hundred and Sixty-three. We came to America when I was eight years old, Anno Domine Seventeen Hundred and Seventy-one. We sailed from Greenoch and after a passage of nine and one-half weeks landed in New York. We came up to Albany and was there some three months. Father there took a lease of some land of Reverend Harry Munro in his patent in Hebron. From Albany we came in a wagon, passing through Salem and to within five miles of Munro's Meadows. The road was not then opened clear through to the Meadows—indeed much of the way there was scarcely any road. We got there in August—the weather very hot and flies and mosquitoes very troublesome. We stopped in a house belonging to Munro until we built one of our own, which was done that fall. Father was very handy with a broad axe and hewed out puncheons for making a floor, a door, et cetera. He that fall did not get any land cleared and sowed with wheat, but having plenty of money bought provisions—probably of Munro.

The only settlers at Munro's Meadows when we got there were Duncan McCall, John McDonald, and Norman and Duncan McCloud. North of us in Granville were a few settlers—at least before the Revolutionary War—two or three brothers of the name of Fisher who were Tories and finally went to Canada, others from Pelham and Palmer in Massachusetts, I think.

We used to go to Salem, seventeen miles, sometimes to meeting and Doctor Clark used to come to preach sometimes at the Meadows, baptizing the children. He was a very pious man.

Never saw Ethan Allen—though I heard much of him— that he made a great deal of trouble driving folks from their land and tearing down their houses. They didn't like him very well. [12]

EARLY LIFE AND WORK

Donald McDonald:

One of the first objects of the settlers was to get a small piece of their land into permanent meadow; and for this purpose some low moist tract was cleared and grubbed as clean as possible and sowed with timothy seed; the seed being got probably in Albany. The farmers generally calculated on having a small piece thus seeded. Each man aimed to have meadow enough to yield sufficient hay to keep one cow through the winter. The first cow which Father owned he bought of Munro for fifteen dollars paying him in days work at three shillings per day.

Pasturing cattle in the summer was a thing then unknown. The cows used to be turned daily into the woods and there get their own keep, browsing upon the twigs and leaves. They used to be furnished with bells. Some would come home regularly at night, others had to be found and drove home. For several years after the first settlement of the country, cattle in the winter were kept on browse mixed with hay. It used to be the prevalent idea that some hay was necessary in order to make the cud for them to chew. Maple and basswood used to be selected for browse for cattle; beech for horses and sheep. Horses could be kept in excellent order on beech browse and grain. Cattle accustomed to browse will eat off basswood twigs as large as a man's finger.

19

In getting the land under cultivation, the early settlers used to cut down the small trees leaving the largest standing and by throwing the brush around them as much as convenient burn them so as to kill them. Burnt trees would not leaf out the next season; those that were girdled would put forth their leaves two and some of them three years after thus shading the ground. The logs of the cut trees were rolled together in heaps often around the standing large trees when convenient and burned. This was all done by hand by the first settlers. There was but one span of horses at Munro's Meadows for six years after I came there. By spring half an acre or an acre more would get cleared by each family and this was sowed with oats and grass seed for meadows.

Wheat was sowed late for they could not get the ground out and burnt over to sow early. From September First to the Twentieth, they endeavored to sow their wheat but often it was not got in till into October. The seed was sowed on the burnt ground without plowing—sowed broadcast—and harrowed in with a half-lap. Some, however, were obliged to hoe in their wheat, teams were so scarce. And it was a good week's work to hoe in an acre. Of course, where a harrow and team could be procured, it made a great savings—and a man could well afford to work such a number of days as were equivalent to the team work in return for such an accommodation.[13]

Eunice Campbell Reid:

In Seventeen Hundred and Seventy-seven there were but two wagons in Argyle township, it was said. One that belonged to Yerry Killmore which he brought with him from Livingston's Manor; the other to "Old" Duncan Campbell. They were common lumber two-horse wagons.

Grain and hay was drawed into the barns on wood-shod sleds and on cars having two small wheels and letting most of the load drag on the ground behind them. They would, however, draw a considerable quantity in this way. Boards were carried on horseback. The first boards in this place were brought up from the Point—two miles—in this way: two bunches were tied together and hung over the backs of the two horses placed one before the other, the forward horse carrying the forward ends by a strap over his back supporting a bunch of boards on each side—the hind horse carrying the hind ends in the same way.[14]

James Bain was born in Columbia County in 1780. His description of the Allen lot in Argyle probably gives a good picture of the typical pioneer homestead.

James Bain:

My father bought Argyle Lot Number Twenty-three in Seventeen Hundred and Eighty-five. The west half of this lot had belonged to Allen and has since belonged to and been cultivated by me. My father died just after he bought and before he moved here. My mother with her six boys then moved up.

There was no clearing on the lot when we first came except that made by Allen towards the northwest corner of the lot amounting to some sixteen acres. Allen had cleared in the first place—after clearing his meadow and putting up his house—a field north of his house in which wheat was sowed in the fall of Seventeen Hundred and Seventy-five. In Seventeen Hundred and Seventy-six this wheat was harvested and a new field on the knoll beyond the meadow south of his house was cleared and sowed with wheat which was ripe when he was murdered. Each of the wheat fields contained about five or six acres and the meadow three or four.

In the spring of Seventeen Hundred and Seventy-seven he had cut over a piece on the rising ground east of the house and meadow, intending evidently to sow this with wheat that fall. So he must have been settled here about two summers before that on which he was killed.

The three apple trees, now old, and the south one decrepid and nearly dead, were set out by Allen and were mere saplings when we came here. The house was of logs and was some eighteen or twenty feet square with the door on its south side and the chimney on the north. Allen had an outdoor oven between the house and the spring. It was about ten rods from the house to the barn.

The nearest neighbors to John Allen at the time of the murder were as follows: Duncan McArthur was nearest of all living two miles east; north three miles was Dugald McKallor; west two and a half miles was old John Beaty; and south-west by west was Neal Gillespie and southwest by south was Archy McNeal—each of their houses being about three miles distant.

The timber originally on the land was mostly oak and chestnut, and west, in the swale beyond the highway, it was all pine—many of the trees of enormous size. [15]

Asa Fitch made this drawing of the Allen house according to the description of Maria McEachron, Mrs. Allen's sister. It shows clearly how small the first pioneer houses were—with the single large bed for both parents and children.

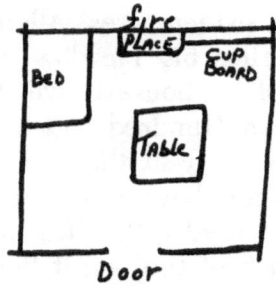

THE ALLEN HOUSE[16]

Samuel Cook (b. 1779) remembered another early house because it, too, had been connected with a murder.

22

Samuel Cook:

The Widow Campbell house [*in Ft. Edward*] was a small house of round logs some fourteen or sixteen feet broad and somewhat greater in length. It stood some years after I came here [*1786*]—well known as the house from which Jane McCrea was taken. It had an old fashioned fireplace in one end—the fireplace was without jambs. There was a loft overhead and a ladder or ladder-like stairs leading to this loft—the stairs being on one side of the fireplace.

The door opened on the east side of the house which was the only entrance. There was a cellar-hole under the house, not walled up. This was entered by a trap door which was rather south of the middle of the floor. Nearly contiguous to the house, in rear of it, was a little woodshed made of slabs, I think. [17]

The "log meeting house" was the first church built in Salem, by Dr. Clark's congregation. It was put up in 1767 when some of the Scotch families were still living in Stillwater.

Donald McDonald:

When I lived with Mister Welch [*c. 1781*], he used to use the old log meeting house for a barn. It stood a little west of where the first framed meeting house was built. It was a large building for this country at that time—forty foot long, I would think. The door was at one end. It was built of round logs and had probably been chinked with mud, et cetera. Think it had no floor—being built ere there was a sawmill in town. It was probably, like most of the other log houses, roofed with black ash bark; though it might have been of oak shingles three or four foot long, like barrel staves, which material was sometimes used. The ash bark was peeled into long strips and flattened by being piled and pressed down with weights upon it till it dried; and then it was placed on the roof—the rough side of the bark being upper most—and held in place by poles running the length of the roof and notched into the end timbers, which were gradually shorter above each other to run the roof up to a ridge. [18]

Robert Blake:

When we came here in the autumn of Seventeen Hundred and Seventy-two, Jacobus O'Bail, a Dutchman, had a gristmill on the east and a sawmill on the west side of Black Creek. This was the first gristmill in town or in this section of country. It was put up for O'Bail by William Reid, had but one run of stones and did but poor work. When William Reid completed his own mill, O'Bail received no more patronage. In Seventeen Hundred and Seventy-two, William Reid had got his mill about completed and they were then putting up the dam when we arrived in the neighborhood. There was at the same time a gristmill at Galesville called Rose's Mill and one at Argyle—Yerry Killmore's. Killmore a few years after rebuilt his mill and I remember we turned out from around here to go over and help him raise it—inhabitants were so few they had to gather them from such great distances to accomplish such a job.

Gilbert Robertson, a Scotchman, was the first settler on Jackson Lot Number Twenty-two and put up a house down towards the kill. He was a wheelwright by trade, but did all kinds of carpentering and was an enterprising man of some property. He was a good workman and was over to Fort Edward one or two years working for the army there—where I used to see him every two or three weeks and let him know how things were going on at home.

24

Robertson, in low water, drove stakes in the kill, put sticks across them and slabs from stick to stick thus making a very convenient footbridge from his house to Archy Livingstons—which, of course, went off with the first high water. Mister More above Salem had put up a similar footbridge a year or two before his. The first bridge for teams to cross was built between old Moses Martin's and McKellip's farms. A few years after this and before the Revolutionary War was closed, a bridge between here and Gilbert Robertson's was built. McKellips and his neighbors was bitterly opposed to our having a bridge here. A great crib, like a log barn, was built up in the middle of the river and long stringers from this to both shores were put on. But before we got the plank on, there came a great flood in the kill and McKellips having a quantity of logs to be sawed at the mills down the kill now rolled them all together into the stream. They came down, piled up against the crib of our bridge and swept it off. Thus we lost our bridge and McKellip lost his logs too for the kill was up so high and furious they could not stop them at the place intended. The bridge lodged at the bend by Mistress McDougall's whence we drawed back part of it—the folks from away down in Cambridge turning out to help us for they felt indignant at McKellips conduct. And the next year we got it completed.[19]

Alexander Livingston's parents came from the same Scotch-Irish colony as the McNeil family. Livingston's mother was the daughter of Alexander McNaughton, first-named proprietor in the Argyle Patent charter, and she had grown up among the Dutch at "Kakiett". Thus Alexander may have been more accustomed to Dutch ways than Scotch ones.

Alexander Livingston:

I remember of being in O'Bails house and mill before he sold to Miller [*before 1776*]. I went to school in a log schoolhouse which stood on the south side of the road just upon the rise of ground in going from the Martin bridge. Whether there was any floor to the schoolhouse, I don't remember, nor anything about the writing benches. The teacher, was one Allen Campbell.

When going there to school I recollect of going one day to O'Bails. He was a Dutchman and the house was all scrubbed neat and nice and everything was in its place—even a linter [*sic*] attached to the house was just as clean as a new pin. O'Bail sold to Miller, a Scotchman, and moved off south somewhere, and again when I went there the cow was in the house and all was dirt, filth, and disorder. I well remember of thinking what a difference there was as to neatness between the Dutch and the Scotch.

The gristmill stood on the east side of the stream, the sawmill on the west side. The mill did not go when I was in it but there were some folks in it getting out some wild hemp that had growed in the mill pond when the water was let off by the dam's getting down. [20]

Tryphena Martin Angel:

I do not remember particularly what houses were standing here [*Fitch's Point, Salem*] when I was a child. There was a number of them—little huts of no consequence. A Scotch family would come into the town and a day or two after would have a little hut or cabin built of logs and covered with bark—without floor, door or chimney—and would thus become resident citizens in a house of their own the day after their arrival. Mother used to hate these Scotch and Irish families that were coming in so unceremoniously. They were all Tories and never ought to have been allowed to come here. [21]

Eunice Campbell Reid:

The Presbyterian Church in Salem used to be called "The New England Church" and Doctor Clark's "The Scotch Church". I remember a preacher was up from New England and preached in the New England Church in the summer when nothing but the roof was on—none of the sides being yet clapboarded. They used to have preaching in it often, though they had no settled minister till long after the war.

I remember well when the church was building. Why it was built I do not know. I never understood that there was any difficulties or disagreements between the New England settlers and Doctor Clark's congregation. When they had no preaching of their own they all used to attend Doctor Clark's meeting.

[Doctor Clark] was a faithful laborer preaching regularly in his church in Salem and often in the towns around in Argyle, Cambridge, and Hebron in different houses, though commonly in barns in the summer season. He did it, too, without pay or nearly so. He had to raise his own potatoes and corn for there were no donation parties in those days, and though some salary was promised him it was never half paid. At length he had to leave here, his support was so inadequate.[22]

Ann McArthur (b. 1770) was the daughter of Duncan McArthur, proprietor of Lot Number 44 of the Argyle Patent. The "Stockbridge Indians" she talks about were a Mohican tribe living in the Stockbridge, Massachusetts area. Many were Christians; a mission to the tribe was begun in the 1730's. Some Stockbridge Indians had fought with the Massachusetts militia in the French and Indian War and many fought for the American side during the Revolutionary War. Sometime between 1785 and 1789, the whole tribe left Stockbridge for western New York State —later they moved farther west.

Ann McArthur:

The Stockbridge Indians used to come into these parts regularly every autumn to hunt, and remain here some weeks till the weather became cool on the close of the Indian summer. They had their wigwams or camps in the woods. There were several in this vicinity. Each company had its own wigwam to which they regularly came.

One of these stood some sixty rods west of here. I remember it well. It was built of small logs about four inches in diameter, slightly notched together at the end—like a toy house though with wide open cracks between the logs—and covered over with bark with a hole in the center for the smoke to escape. Their fire was built on the ground in the middle, and three sides were occupied with seats or beds made up by a layer of pine boughs broken from the ends of the limbs, and over this a layer of straw. The Indians, wrapped in their blankets, would then lay on the straw with their heads toward the outer wall and their feet toward the fire—the fourth side of the wigwam being occupied by the doorway. About a dozen occupied this wigwam coming here every autumn to hunt the

deer, bear, raccoon, et cetera. We never used to have any fear of them but were always on friendly terms. An old squaw I used to have some degree of affection for; her name was Rebekah Kack-Kees-Moh.

I well remember on one occasion when I was a little girl our folks had borrowed a knife of the Indians to do some butchering with that day. About dusk the squaw came to our house and wanted to get a bundle of straw. Father told her to go to the barn and get what she wanted. When our folks had got through with the knife they sent me to carry it home. I went to the hut, pushed aside the blanket and went in. Rebekah was not there, and I then felt alarmed at perceiving they were all strangers to me. So I handed them the knife and made my way out and homeward as fast as convenient. On the way, I met Rebekah carrying her bundle of straw and told her I had been to her hut and that I was scared when I found she was not there. She hereupon laughed heartily.

I remember an Indian once came to our house and wanted the loan of a frying pan. He had to motion a long time ere our folks could understand what he wanted—showing that it was long and circular at one end and to be put on the fire and then making a spluttering noise with his mouth exactly resembling the frying of meat. We at once understood him and got him the utensil. He put the meat which he brought with him into the pan and cooked it over the fire and ate it. He then poured some of the grease from the pan onto his hands and rubbed them until they were well and evenly anointed all over. Then stepping to the fireplace, he drew his hands along the chimney-back till the palms were well covered with soot. He next rubbed the palms of his hands together until the soot was mixed with the grease. He now commenced rubbing his face with his hands, stepping up to the looking-glass to see that he got all parts of his face evenly covered. This being done, with his fingers spread slightly apart he drew the ends of them along his face lengthwise, thus leaving regular stripes of black and flesh color over his whole face. The same motion was next repeated crosswise of his face— thus cutting the stripes up into squares somewhat like a checkerboard. Having thus finished, he turned to us and smiling said "War! War!" and then left the house.[23]

Donald McDonald was only eleven or twelve years old when he left home to work for Mister Bell.

Donald McDonald:

When I first went from home in search of some place to live and support myself, I went to Mister Bell's, a Scotchman who lived east of where Colin McFarland now lives. A hurricane had blown down all the trees on a small piece of Bell's land and I assisted Bell in cutting up the trees. Bell got a new light axe for me and used the old one for himself and I well remember I could easily cut off the tree at its butt, and ere Bell who would take the next cut above me would get his off, I would go on to the third cut and get that off before him. Bell repeatedly telling me, "My child, ye need not work so fast!"

I fared very well at Bell's and it would have been well had I remained there, but Father not knowing I had obtained a place, meeting Armstrong, made a bargin with him to have me work for him a year.

The winter of Seventeen Hundred and Eighty was the hardest ever known in this country. For three months the eves never dropped from the houses, the cold was so severe and steady and the snow was full four feet deep, I presume, all that time. I lived that winter with Captain John Armstrong who resided north of Salem Village—Lot Number One Hundred and Thirty-one. It was the hardest winter that a poor boy ever had. He had four horses, four cows, four calves, two or three young cattle and twelve sheep—and about half enough hay to winter them on. It was my work to take care of the stock and provide firewood for the family. He was away from home about all the time frolicking around with his companions. I used daily to tread a path from the barn west over the flat to the hill which was then covered with wood; then cut down a tree; trample the snow down all around the top of it; cut off the limbs and lay them along the path for the cattle, et cetera, to eat; then drive them out to the spot and let them go to feeding; then get up the team, snake the butt of the tree to the house and cut it up for firewood.

I thus carried all his stock through the winter on browse, cutting over some three or four acres of woods taking all except the largest trees. The wood was all beech, maple and basswood; there were no pines or hemlocks or tamaracks growing along Beaver Brook. Of course for a boy I was constantly employed. But this I should not have minded had I been furnished with suitable fare. Armstrong was a liberal, generous man, but he was little of the time at home and knew not how his wife treated me. My main diet was mush and milk, the milk skimmed—and not only skimmed but profusely watered—ere it was brought onto the table for me. I thus fell away so that I did not appear like the same child in the course of three or four months, and should probably have died had I continued there.

Father becoming aware of how hard I was faring at Armstrong's took me from him, and I next lived with Joseph Welch where my situation was as easy and comfortable as it had previously been hard and laborious.[24]

It is nice to know that Donald McDonald was well-treated in two out of the three places where he worked. Many of the boys and girls "bound out" by their parents probably weren't very happy with their lots. McDonald knew a boy at Munro's Meadows named Robert McNight who "was a bound boy to Harry Munro and enlisted into the service to free him from his indentures and was killed only a few months after." *At the taking of Fort Ann* "he was the first one that went out of the fort and was shot down by the Indians or Tories, I suppose, after the surrender"[25]

PART TWO:

WAR

First Shots

Accounts of the war years tell of a bitter, civil war-type struggle in the county. The New England settlers of Turner's Patent turned Salem into a Whig town—very early driving out some Tory Methodists settled just south in Camden Valley (today part of the town of Salem) plus individual Tories like John Cloughlin. The "Yankees" carried most of Salem's new Scotch-Irish settlers along with them politically, and many like Alexander McNish served in the militia.

Things were different in Argyle and the tiny settlement at Munro's Meadows. There, the people were neutrals or Tory sympathizers—not because they were new immigrants (most of the Argyle proprietors had lived all their adult lives in this country) but probably as a result of the feud with Ethan Allen and his Green Mountain Boys over the "New Hampshire Grants." New Scotch settlers, holding New York deeds or leases, had been Allen's main victims in his border war of 1770–1775. Though the New York-granted Turner Patent also lay in the disputed territory, Allen never attacked this town which was founded and first settled by fellow "Yankees."

Sarah McCoy McNish was born in "1752 or '53" in Ireland. When she was two years old the family emigrated to America. They arrived in Salem (then "White Creek" or "New Perth" according to the different names given the town by the New England and Scotch settlers) between 1765 and 1767. Sarah married Alexander McNish in 1778.

Sarah McCoy McNish:

John Barnes commanded one of the most active scouting parties of the country during the Revolutionary War. He owned and lived on Lot Number Fifty-two. [*Later*] he sold this to Nathaniel Carswell and took his pay in continental money which depreciated so in value that it about ruined him.

35

In his company were the following persons: Alexander McNish, Robert and Captain John Armstrong—their brother Major Thomas perhaps also belonged to it and also James their remaining brother though he was by no means a man of the spirit and activity of his three brothers—Isaac Lyttle of Hebron, Robert Boyd, Esquire Livingston of Hebron. Several others also belonged to the party. Often but part of the company were out—the number called on depending on the service in which they were at different times engaged.

One John Cloughlin, by trade a cooper at the breaking out of the Revolutionary War, was living, I believe, on Lot Number Three. He was so warm a loyalist that it was determined to capture him if possible. The party under Barnes proceeded by night to his house. There was an entryway through which they had to pass to get into the main room of the house. Coming into this entryway awoke him so that as they flung open the inner door, he was discerned escaping out at the window. They fired upon him, but probably without wounding him severely as he made off into the woods.

His wife screamed and cried so violently that she would not hush on their trying to quiet her by words, and they clenched hold of her and shook her to stop her noise. Cloughlin was never seen in the town after this and his wife also disappeared soon after—doubtless joining him and going off together to Canada.[26]

36

The attack on Skenesborough by the Salem scout and other Washington County men took place on the same night as Ethan Allen's taking of Ticonderoga (as planned by Allen and Arnold). Skene was Public Enemy Number One as far as most Washington County Whigs were concerned—because of his active schemes to develop his "aristocratic" estate and extend his power in the county. In 1777, Salem Whig "Hugh More went into Baum's camp on purpose to get a chance to shoot old Skene, but he did not succeed."[27]; The attack on Skene's home was made before he had actually taken sides politically and when he was still on his way home from a trip to England. The Salem scout and/or William McNish weren't aware of this last fact.

William was the second son of Sarah and Alexander McNish.

William McNish:

About the same time [*as the attack on Cloughlin*], Barnes' company was ordered out to proceed to Skenesborough and capture Lord Skene. Father, the two Armstrongs, Isaac Lyttle, et cetera were at this time with Barnes. Intending to approach there in the dead of night, they did not start till afternoon. When darkness overtook them they had twelve miles farther to go. A double sentry guarded Skene's house, a fact which they were not aware of. A sentry was placed at the house and another half a mile distant on the road. Before they were suspicious that caution was necessary, a gun was fired toward the residence of Skene. Knowing the alarm was now given they started forward at their utmost speed. At the same instant, another gun was fired at the house. They rushed on and surrounded the house on all sides.

Some of their number now searched the house thoroughly—but Skene had escaped. They supposed he had fled into the woods when the alarm was first given. They found the corpse of his wife in a small apartment partitioned off in the cellar. It was laid in a very nice wooden coffin, superior to anything which the carpenters of the country could make. And this was enclosed in a lead coffin which was sealed and soldered up so as to render it quite air tight. His wife had a

37

legacy left her of a certain sum per day whilst she was above ground, and Skene had placed her there to receive this legacy.

On opening it [*the coffin*] the corpse was found but little changed. The coffin must have been purchased in Montreal or Quebec. The corpse was taken out and buried. The lead was too much needed for bullets to be buried, and it, together with the choice liquors found in the cellar, was delivered over to the commissaries of the continental army. There were about forty Negroes of both sexes upon the premises and these were about the only occupants they found. These Negroes were all full-blooded Africans, save one, a girl six or eight years old named Sylvia who claimed Skene for her father. Captain Barnes brought her home with him on his return. She remained in this town and died but a few years ago.[28]

Skene may have had a natural daughter among his servants, but the other scandal related here—about keeping his wife's corpse in order to collect a legacy—is certainly false. This story was widely told and accepted at the time, though. Jacob Bitely, the son of a Whig family, tells us the tale again below. And George Webster, the son of Colonel Alexander Webster—though he was only seven years old at the time of the raid—can definitely state: "I have full faith in his ⟨Skene's⟩ having left his wife unburied to receive money thereby."[29] *But Robert Blake, a "Protectioner", gives a more sensible explanation:* "Skene had placed his wife after her decease in the cellar in a lead coffin with her rings and her jewelry all upon her for the purpose of having her carried back to Scotland or Ireland—wherever she was from—to be there interred among her kindred. And the Americans when they captured Skene's mansion rifled the coffin of everything that was valuable, and what they did with the corpse I do not know."[30]

Jacob Bitely did not move to present-day Washington County until 1778. But his early memories of Fort Ticonderoga and vicinity have an importance and interest for the story of this

38

county. The "Swisher" mentioned here was one Peter Switzer who is named on both British payroll lists and American prisoner of war lists as commissary of the Ticonderoga garrison.

Jacob Bitely:

I was born in New Jersey, November Ninth, Seventeen Hundred and Sixty-two. About the year Seventeen Hundred and Sixty-five, my father moved from Jersey to Lake Champlain. He settled on the lake shore, on the south line of the town of Bridport, Vermont. He took a lease for twenty-one years on two hundred acres of land here from Robert Ross of the City of New York. Ross, I think, had served in the French War and received these lands for military services—all the lands along there were soldiers rights, and the title to them was thus derived directly from the Crown, and was regarded as more secure than any other title. There was a great fuss, I remember, about all the lands there, but we nor our neighbors were never molested—the chief troubles being close up to the foot of the mountains, some ways east and south of us. Our house was seven miles north of Ticonderoga on the lake shore.

I well remember the taking of Ticonderoga at the breaking out of the war. De La Place, an old fellow no better than an old goose, had charge of the fort which was garrisoned by some thirty or forty old men and cripples that were worn out in their country's service. Swisher was the commissary's name.

He was sixty or seventy years old, and my brother Peter, two years and two months older than me, was living in the fort with the commissary at this time. There was a woman whom they called Rosa also living in the fort—she washed for the soldiers and had an equivocal reputation. She was a great favorite with the commissary for a while, till he got mad at her for something and in a rage kicked her outdoors. There might have been one or two other females about the fort.

I used to know Mister Beman very well and his boys Nathan and Samuel were often with us playing ball, et cetera. Boys were so scarce we had to go considerable distances for playmates. When Ethan Allen and his men came, Nathan Beman went with others over to where the battoes lay, got them without the slightest alarm, took them over to the Vermont side. Allen and as many man as they could carry embarked and crossed to the fort with muffled oars. Nathan Beman then showed them the way to the little gate . . .

Brother Peter was in bed with the commissary at this time, awakened by the noise, he asked what was the matter. Swisher, who had sprung up and was in his shirt flaps looking out the window replied: "The rebels have taken the fort." "The rebels, who are they?" "The Yankees," Swisher replied. The stores of the fort were thrown open and "help yourselves to what you like boys" was the word; the visitors drank freely and had quite a jolly time. What was done with the prisoners or where they were sent I do not know. Brother Peter was well known to several of the captors, and known to be a friend to them and their cause, and was left free to come home.

When Whitehall was taken, Skene I guess was absent in Montreal. He used to be away from home much of the time, passing to and fro in a little sloop which he owned upon the lake and which was manned by two or three of his blacks. I remember this sloop used to pass our house often and the Negroes landed at our house to get some milk, two of them coming ashore. Skene was not then on board.[31]

Battoes or batteaux were a specific type of river craft. Isaac Dickison of Stillwater (b. 1768) gives this definition: "Battoes were flat-bottomed boats about six feet wide and thirty feet long built with a regular curve from the middle to the sides and not with an angle or knees such as our skiffs have. It took three men to navigate each battoe—two to row or pole and one to steer."[32]

The naval battle Bitely speaks of was the Battle of Valcour Island, October 11, and the follow-up engagement off Crown Point on the 13th.

Jacob Bitely:

I think there is some mistake in our histories as to the date of the naval battle on Lake Champlain in Seventeen Hundred and Seventy-six. My recollection is quite strong that we were haying at the time, and therefore that it must have been in August. The men, having blowed up their boats to prevent their falling into the hands of the British, fled along the shore of the lake, passing and many of them stopping at our house. They were so black with the smoke of the powder that they could scarcely to be told from Negroes, and their clothes were all blackened and marked with the burnt powder of the guns.

Carleton following on after the Americans, landed his Indians on Mister Richardson's farm, and the regulars opposite to it on Put's Creek [*Putnam Creek*]. He advanced hence to Kirby's Point within three miles of Ticonderoga, but durst go no nearer. To take the fort by assault could not be done, it was put in such a state of defense. Whole acres around the fort were set with pickets and sharpened stakes or covered with fallen trees—so that he could not approach the walls with any order to scale them. So he returned to Canada, burning the few buildings around Crown Point. The fort there had

41

been previously burned. All the neighborhood around Crown Point was wholly deserted by both parties through the following winter. I remember of being up there in "pigeon time" that fall hunting, and everybody was gone from around there.[33]

Elizabeth Conkey Pratt (b. 1769) was the daughter of Joshua Conkey who like many other settlers was a veteran of the French and Indian War.

Elizabeth Conkey Pratt:

In the Revolutionary War, Father was commissary for the Salem Regiment and Mother did the baking for the troops when they were mustered in Salem. Our oven was outdoors and she had often to bake three oven-fulls of bread per day. Always before putting bread into the oven Father would with his gun take a walk about the surrounding woods to see that there was no enemy lurking about to steal the bread.

We had frequent alarms on the approach of the enemy, when the families would fly from their houses to the woods. Three guns fired in quick succession at the Salem Fort was the signal to all within their hearing that danger was near. [*Once*] a man, having a gun on his shoulder, was driving a lot of hogs out of a cornfield up Black Creek. Somebody saw him and heard the rustling and saw the moving among the corn and supposed a large number of the enemy were making their way through the cornfield. He ran and gave the alarm. Mother heard the three guns fired in the village. Soon Joseph Slarrow came riding by at full speed exclaiming "Aunt Dinah, fly from your house—a large body of the enemy are up by

Captain McNitt's." Two or three other runners soon passed giving the same intelligence. Mother had a large batch of bread kneaded up which she was loath to leave to spoil. She ran up and met Mistress McCracken coming over the bridge from her house. They concluded if the danger became imminent, their husbands who were at the village would speedily fly home and aid them in getting away. Every family in town forsook their homes during this night except ours and McCracken's. In the evening Father and McCracken came home and told us it was a false alarm.[34]

Eunice Campbell Reid:

An itinerant minister came along in the wartime and preached in a barn from the text "I will go and return to my first husband for then it was better with me than now"—Hosea, Chapter Two, Verse Seven. Though he did not apply it to the political condition of the country, some of the Whigs in Salem were so firey that they denounced him as a Jesuit, a Tory in disguise, et cetera. Where he was from or what his name was, I do not know.

And so of Doctor Clark, who took no active part with either side but advised everyone as he thought was for their good and wished to be regarded by every individual as his friend and well-wisher. He was denounced by the Whigs as a Tory and by the Tories as a rebel so that he often used to say he felt it to be slippery ground on which he was standing.

One Sabbath I remember all the men came to meeting armed with loaded muskets so fearful were they that they would be attacked. The dogs—they too used to be allowed to come to meeting then—probably smelt the powder of the guns, for they kept howling and barking around the church all the time. It was the most doleful meeting I ever attended.

Soldiers were quartered in the New England Church all the time Burgoyne was here. It was burned soon after the military had ceased to be quartered there—probably in the year Seventeen Hundred and Seventy-eight. It was always said that it was burned by the Tories.[35]

COMING OF BURGOYNE

Burgoyne's invasion army reached the vicinity of the Bitely homestead on June 30, 1777. Richardson's farm was the second one north of the Bitely's.

Jacob Bitely:

Burgoyne in Seventeen Hundred and Seventy-seven landed on precisely the same spots where Carleton landed the year before—his Indians on Richardson's farm and his regulars at Put's Creek on the flats bordering the creek. He laid here some time, I should think two or three weeks. Parties of the Indians were out every day scouting and hunting through the woods. They were always uttering "Curse on the Bostonians" in their grum [*sic*] voice whenever we met them; and this was the only English expression they appeared to have learned. They did not molest us or any of the families about there—we being non-combatants and unarmed. My brothers John and Henry had volunteered into the militia and were away from home at this time and indeed through the whole of this year.[36]

A few days before landing his army north of the Bitely farm, Burgoyne had issued a proclamation to the inhabitants of "New York, New Hampshire, and New England" calling on them to stay quietly on their farms and to put tokens on their hats and their cattle's horns showing they were loyal to the King. (The loyalist token was a bit of white paper; the Whigs wore sprigs of evergreen.) Burgoyne also offered "Protection" to all coming into his camp.

Isabel MacIntyre:

The year before Burgoyne came down, all the men were training a great deal of the time. Some were for the King and some against him. When Burgoyne arrived at Skenesborough all the families from Munro's Meadows went there in a company together to obtain protection—not from the Indians, for the Indians hadn't joined him then. We hid our beds and other things in thick bushes leaving nothing in the houses when we went away. We found these things all safe and undisturbed when we got back. We started for Skenesborough in the morning; we went on foot driving our cattle with us. Father had one horse, three milch cows and two steers. We followed a path through the woods; got to Skenesborough the same day, the distance being seventeen miles. The settlers there had fled leaving their houses empty; there was but a few houses there at that time. Skene's stone house and barn I remember very well.

We occupied one of the vacant houses. There were not many families that came in there to take protection, and we were not crowded in our accommodations, and there was no sickness or deaths whilst we were there. We slept upon blankets on the floor, not having any beds with us. The army had their tents pitched, under which they slept, and they were training every day. It was a large army. Our cattle ran at large and the fields of grain were all trampled down and destroyed. We sold the milk to the soldiers every day—they commonly coming to us for it, but sometimes we carried it to them.

I remember of seeing the water of the lake there, but do not remember of seeing any relicts of the boats run ashore and burned. The English army at length struck their tents and marched away from the place. Then a large army of Hessians passed through after them. The troops having thus all gone from the place we returned home; we were there about five weeks. None of the men from the Meadows went to join the army on either side.[37]

Donald McDonald and his son John II tell of John McDonald I's difficult position in the wartime. There is every reason to believe them about John Sr.'s service with Barnes' Rangers late in the War—since Donald went to live in the house of the Whig John Armstrong in 1779–80. But did John McDonald really "stop upon the way" to Skenesborough in 1777?

Donald McDonald:

At the time Burgoyne reached Skenesborough the five old Scottish families which formed the settlement at Munro's Meadows started to go to his camp to take protection—but my father, John McDonald, stopped upon the way from some cause, I do not know what, and did not go there with our family.

Father was one of the rangers belonging to Captain Barnes company of Salem, and was out several times upon scouting service—mostly in the last years of the war, I suppose. They went to see if Indians had come up the lake from Canada and on similar services—whenever a report of this kind got abroad. The country was often alarmed by stories of this kind.[38]

John McDonald II:

Grandfather would gladly have remained neutral in the Revolution, but this was not permitted, and after deliberation he enlisted in Captain Barnes' Rangers. This saved him from being harried by the Whigs, and his nationality probably saved him from such of the Tories as were Scotch—as many of that nationality were in and about Hebron, where Grandfather settled.[39]

While the McIntyres and others were joining the army at Skenesborough, some Whig families were already fleeing in the opposite direction.

George Webster:

My father Alexander Webster was born in Argyleshire in the north of Scotland in Seventeen Hundred and Thirty-four. When a young man he went into the south county of Scotland for a time, and thence into England where he lived six years and then embarked for America at Whitehaven in Seventeen Hundred and Seventy-two. I was born in England, August, Seventeen Hundred and Sixty-nine. Father had seven children, five of which reached maturity. Two were born in Scotland, two in England and three in this country. One child died on the passage over the ocean. Father landed in New York and came thence direct to Salem where he lived two years on a farm up White Creek, next north the Cleveland farm. Whilst in Salem he was elected onto the Committee of Safety for the town. He then moved into Hebron in the McClellan neighborhood where he resided through the war. He was here captain and afterwards major and colonel in the militia in time of the war. In Seventeen Hundred and Seventy-seven he was the representative of Charlotte County in the Provincial Congress or Legislature.

When Burgoyne reached Skenesborough the Hebron settlers fled down into Salem and stayed with their Salem friends two or three weeks when that town was also evacuated. Our furniture, et cetera, was secreted in a by-nook beside Black Creek and covered over with brush. The Tories did not find it. Munro's settlers in the north part of the town came down and took possession of our evacuated dwellings—living in them in our absence, fondly hoping to have them for their own when the country was conquered by the King.

We were at Hugh More's near Sodom a few days and thence went south across More's bridge, a rickety structure, tipped and slanting almost as steep as a house roof in some places. I do not remember how we travelled, whether on foot or on horseback, but have a faint impression of having rode some of the way in a cart. We came to Albany and thence to Esopus, going all the way by land, Father having to be here to attend the Provincial Legislature at this time. Some other families from Salem accompanied us. McKnight was one of them and continued on from Esopus out into Pennsylvania to some connection of his wife. McCarter from Salem also was with us with his family. We were staying at Esopus when it was burnt by the British—Father being in the Legislature in the village and his family ten miles north. We saw the light of the burning buildings very distinctly, and the Dutch matrons in the neighborhood where we were made a great clamor on seeing the light. Father was pursued by some British soldiers in the street at Esopus but eluded them by turning aside down a by-street.

He returned to Salem in the fall in season to dig his potatoes; he did not move his family back until the latter part of winter. In the spring, I remember, we burnt the meadows over to make them smooth for mowing—the grass not having been cut from them the year before.[40]

Tryphena Martin Angel:

In the war [Father] was away from home when the families evacuated the town. He was either in the army or away with a scouting party and so was not here to aid us in getting away. We lived then in a log house halfway from the present red house to the kill.

I remember little about our flight except as I have heard it told by my mother and others. The town was full of exaggerated and alarming reports. Burgoyne was at Whitehall and it was said he had a hundred thousand soldiers with him—British, Hessians, and Indians—and was coming down through this place and would kill every enemy of the King.

48

Daniel Livingston was living at that time in a house of Father's down near where the old bridge across the kill was. He helped us to get away. Some of our things were buried, others sunk in the well, and the rest were put into the ox-cart in which Aaron and Miriam rode, Livingston driving the oxen. Mother rode on the old mare and I was tied on behind her or had to hold on to her. We forded the kill above where the bridge was afterwards built. We kept down by the Jackson ponds and by Joseph Heustis' tavern and on down through Cambridge and Sancoick to one Brown's in Hoosic, a mile or so beyond Sancoick, where we stayed. I think Father had previously arranged with Brown to keep us. [*Sancoick had disappeared by the mid-nineteenth century. George Fowler describes it as having been* "just south of the present (1847) line of the county in Hoosic where is a fall of some twenty feet in the stream. It was also called Rensselaer's Mill—John VanRensselaer being the owner of the gristmill there."][41]

I was so young that I remember nothing whatever of this journey except one incident. It is this. On the road somewhere toward Hoosic was a large slough hole or brook across which poles were laid to keep the horses, et cetera from miring in it. The foot of the horse we rode got caught between these poles so that she fell pitching Mother and me off into the mud. We were not hurt but badly frightened and sadly besmeared with muck and mud. A few days after our arrival at Brown's my brother Moses was born. We came back before cold weather.

Daniel Livingston did not move his family away. He wanted to be perfectly neutral and the neutrals and Tories all stayed at home. The Scotch and Irish generally were Tories. William Reid was a Tory and did not move his family away. Daniel Livingston afterwards moved to Argyle now Greenwich where his remaining life was spent, this side of Reid's Corners. A blind woman owned a lot of land there which she gave to Daniel Livingston to move there and take care of her during her life.

As already stated, part of our things were buried in time of the retreat before Burgoyne: pots and kettles, a large brass

kettle, pewter platters and other dishes, the iron trammel that hung in the chimney. When we got back we found all these things had been stolen by the Tories. We never got any trace as to who it was that had taken them. Mother used to most strongly suspect Bowman of being the culprit. Bowman lived in Jackson next beyond McKellips. His children that I remember were John, Samuel, Betty, and Peggy. Peggy was a fine singer. She used to work at Father's spinning flax, et cetera and Father used to get her to sing the songs she knew often, particularly "Granny O'Wale" and other Whig songs of that day.[42]

THE MURDERS

On July 25, 1777, two horrible incidents suddenly changed the nature of the war for people in the county. One or more parties of Burgoyne's Indians killed a whole family, the Allens, in Argyle and later in the day murdered a young girl, Jane McCrea, just outside Fort Edward. At this time, Burgoyne and his army were encamped part way between Fort Ann and Fort Edward.

THE ALLEN FAMILY

John Bain:

John Allen was son-in-law of George—or Yerry, for he was always called by this his Dutch name, Yerry being the Dutch for George—Killmore. Killmore owned the mills at Argyle Corners a little ways up the Moses Kill. He had a gristmill there. He had three sons, Adam, Simon, and Henry and two girls besides the two killed—namely Elizabeth and Maria, widow of Peter McEachron.[43]

Maria McEachron was eighteen years old and recently married at the time of her sisters' murders.

Maria McEachron:

My father, Yerry Killmore, told my brother Adam to go and help Allen get in his wheat, but Adam felt lazy and wouldn't go, and Father used afterwards to say he could forgive Adam for all his disobedience, he was so glad he disobeyed him at this time. So he sent his Negro Tom, who was a young man grown, in Adam's place, and the wench Sarah, who was about twelve years old, and my sister Catherine also went along. They went on foot early on Saturday morning and were to return home at night.

51

They wrought together in the harvest field, Mistress Allen binding the sheaves, the black girl carrying them together, Allen and Tom reaping, and Catherine at the house taking care of the babe and getting their dinner—she having gone for this purpose, that Mistress Allen might help in the wheatfield. To make more sure of killing all, it was supposed the Indians lurking in the woods waited till they should be all in the house at dinner, for twas then that the attack was made.

Catherine and the Negroes not coming home at night, on Sunday morning Father sent the boy Abram, Tom's brother, on horseback. Catherine was lame in one foot at this time and he sent the horse for her to ride home on—not knowing but what her foot might have got worse from walking and thus prevented her coming home the night before.

[*After coming upon the scene of the massacre*] Abram jumped on the horse and rode homewards, three miles to McKallors—choked and crying, he could scarcely for a time make out to them the tale. He durst not ride any further. They thought at first he was afraid of the Indians in the woods and had lied to them about the family's being murdered as an excuse for his fears, and to get them to send somebody home with him.

Allen was found on the path to the barn and near to the barn. A piece behind him was Catherine; behind her and half way from the house to the barn was Mistress Allen with her babe in her arms and placed at her breast—where it must have been put by the Indians, for to scalp it they must have had it out of its mother's arms. The two children and the Negro girl had tried to hide themselves in the bed, for they were found there, the bedclothes gashed and bloody from the tomahawks. Blood was tracked all around the floor. Bullet holes were perforated through the door, and there was one bullet through the cupboard door in the northeast corner of the house.

I was living with my husband, Peter McEachron, at the head of the lake [*Cossayuna*]. On that Saturday he was over at Salem helping them put up pickets around the Presbyterian Church, and came home at night. The next day, Sunday, we heard of the murder and fearing our house would be sought out and we be murdered, we forsook it and in our two boats went onto the island in the lake where we stayed all night, not venturing to kindle a fire lest it should reveal our hiding place to the Indians.

Next day some of our neighbors passing saw our house deserted. Alarmed, they called our names walking along the lake shore. Hearing and seeing who they were, we answered and came ashore. Cheered up by them, we concluded it was better to stay at home and defend our house if attacked, than forsake it and thus invite its being destroyed.[44]

Daniel Smith (b. 1769) was living at the house of his grandfather Duncan Taylor at the time of the massacre—about four miles from the Allen house.

Daniel Smith:

When John McDougall and James Gillis heard the news they doubted whether it was true and went down to Allen's house to see. Finding it was true, they jumped onto Allen's horses and rode back. Allen's family was not buried that day. It was Sunday. All were too much concerned for their own safety and too poorly furnished with arms and ammunition to venture down there to bury them that day. To add to our terror and alarm, word came from Fort Edward towards night that the Widow Campbell, such was the report we first got, had just been murdered and scalped by the Indians.

All the families around there gathered together on Sunday night at James Gillis's house. It was about a mile north of Yerry Killmore's. A part of the men stood guard around the house through the night. It had been resolved to go down and bury the Allen family the next forenoon. And to be more equipped for this hazardous business, John McDougall kindled a fire out in the yard and was all night casting bullets and buckshot—melting up most of the pewter dishes about the house for this purpose.

The next forenoon, viz. Monday forenoon, the young men rode down to bury the Allen family. Mister Killmore and his two youngest boys went. Simon, his oldest son, was absent from home down in Livingston's Manor at this time. John, Alexander, and Archy Gillis went to the burial, also John and perhaps Peter Gilchrist, Alexander and John Taylor and several others whose names I cannot recall. They rode down all of them on horseback carrying their guns. Some of the bodies had been torn and mangled by Allen's hogs. Allen had a bullet shot through his body.[45]

JANE MC CREA

It is possible that Jane McCrea was more or less accidentally killed by an American bullet instead of by the Indians who were taking her into Burgoyne's camp—supposedly at the direction of her fiance', a loyalist officer. Mrs. McNeil later claimed that this is what happened, and the following accounts in some ways suggest this too. But the fact that Burgoyne, himself, always believed the Indians had committed the murder is powerful evidence for the opposite case. Gerald Howson's Burgoyne of Saratoga, *(New York, 1979) has an interesting discussion of all the evidence on this question.*

Mrs. McNeil and the "Widow Campbell" were one and the same person. Campbell was the name of her first husband; McNeil that of her last.

Robert Blake:

I have often heard Mistress Sarah McNeil tell of her and Miss Jane McCrea's capture and flight toward Burgoyne's camp.

She [*Mrs. McNeil*] was sixty or seventy years old at the time, and had buried three husbands. She was a large fat woman with a good deal of vanity and pride about her. Her maiden name was Fraser, and she claimed to be a cousin of General Fraser of Burgoyne's army. Her house stood, say forty rods from the fort, up the river a few rods from the river and a few rods from the main road.

Jane McCrea lived with her brother Colonel John McCrea. They lived at that time on the west side of the river, several miles below Fort Edward. Miss McCrea left her brother's house voluntarily and came to Mistress McNeil's hoping for a chance to get from there into the British camp.

Miss McCrea and Mistress McNeil were, as the latter has often told me, sitting outside of the door in the shade on the north side of the house, it being a warm summer's day, engaged in sewing. A party of American soldiers had passed along the road and up the hill a short time before, and their going out had been observed by the ladies, and they had expressed their wishes that them fellows "might get a scattering before they came back." Sitting there and sewing, they were in rather a jocular way conversing when all at once there was a rattling of musket shots among the bushes on the hillside about half a mile distant; and soon emerging from the bushes they descried the party of Americans pursued hotly by a band of Indians. Alarmed, the ladies ran into the house. As the combatants came on rushing confusedly along the road, to their consternation, some half a dozen Indians separated from the party and made directly for the house. Some of them held of each others' hands, jumping and yelling as they leaped forwards toward the house.

Terror-stricken, they raised a trap-door in the floor and jumped into a small cellar-hole under it—Miss McCrea, Mistress McNeil, and a younger man about twenty years old named Norman Morrison. A Negress and her children were the only other persons about the house. The wench with her children got partly through the trap door, when Mistress McNeil pushed her back, telling her there was not room for her there, and thereupon pulled down the trap door. The wench hereupon send [*sic*] up stairs with her children, and there found a more secure hiding-place than her mistress, for the Indians did not go into the chamber.

Instantly they rushed into the house and probably perceived some motion to the trap door, for they ran directly to it, pulled it up, reached down with their hands, grasped the young man and ladies by their hair and pulled them up through the trap door. Morrison has often told me how they lifted him out of the cellar by the hair on his head. An Indian on each side of Morrison grasped his arms, locked theirs in with his and ran out with him and up the hill. An Indian on each side of Mistress McNeil ran her off in the same way, whilst others placed Miss McCrea in the saddle of the horse and taking hold of the reins ran as fast as they could—for by this time the American party having gained the fort and given the alarm, several companies were drawn up outside the fort and paraded upon the green and commenced firing at the Indians. [*This was the last Mrs. McNeil or Morrison saw of Jane.*]

They fired by platoons, as Morrison told me, and instantly as a platoon fired, the Indians would all drop flat upon the ground—that the bullets might pass over them—ordering Morrison to do the same and pulling him down with them as often as they fell. Then jumping up, they would run at their utmost speed till another platoon fired. Thus they scampered up the hill. Morrison being lightest of foot was ahead of the ladies. Mistress McNeil being large and fat could not run to advantage, but the two Indians, one on each side of her holding her arms, pulled her along as fleetly as possible. Mistress McNeil was so exhausted with the race that she was scarcely able to stand when they reached the camp. How far this was, I don't know. Probably two miles or more from her house.

As soon as the Indians were out of sight up the hill, the six hundred American troops at Fort Edward evacuated the fort and retreated down the river to Schuylerville. The British and Tories sneered at this cowardly act—their making no attempt to defend themselves. There were a number of Americans killed by the Indians in the encounter that first alarmed Mistress McNeil. These were gathered up by the British a few days after, and buried just at the foot of the hill near the edge of the bushes. I was passing there to my Uncle Bell's when the British soldiers were gathering up the bodies to bury them or rather to burn them, for they covered them over with logs and wood of pitch pine and set the logs on fire to char and partly consume the bodies, so that they would not taint the air—this was their only object—but for this they would not have touched them I suppose. They were covered up with their clothes on, and when burning, the explosion of their cartridges was repeatedly heard as the fire reached them.

She [*Jane McCrea*] was not buried by the Americans, for they had all fled, but by the Tories in the neighborhood. My uncle's folks assisted in her burial and showed me her grave only a few days after it.

I have repeatedly heard her [*Mrs. McNeil*] tell how the Indians held of her arms and made her run, they running like grey-hounds and dragging her along and that she was tired all but to death ere she got to the camp. When Burgoyne lay at Fort Edward, Archy Livingston, my father, and all the other families around here went over to get protection from Burgoyne. We were there over a week. I stayed during the time at my Uncle Bell's. Mistress McNeil put up at his house all the time I was there and I knew her well. She used to go down every day from Uncle's to visit her cousin General Fraser, who with the other officers had their headquarters at Smith's House. This was a large house just below the fort. It was afterwards surrounded by pickets.

Mistress McNeil was talking a great deal at that time about houses that belonged to her in New York City—whether she really had any houses there and was really a cousin to General Fraser, I do not know—and was telling how she was going to give the use of such a house to this officer and such a house to that for their quarters on their arrival in New York— for that they would reach New York was a fixed fact at that time.

Norman Morrison was a Highlander, about twenty years old at this time. He was with the army some little time. And I have often heard him say that whenever he met either of the Indians that aided in running him into the camp, they recognized him and would give a grunt and smile and shake hands with him.[46]

Mary Gillespie Bain was born in 1770, the daughter of Neal Gillespie, one of the original proprietors of the Argyle Patent.

Mary Gillespie Bain:

Mistress McNeil of Fort Edward was an old fat woman, sixty years old or more I should think. She was Scotch and spoke considerably broad. I have heard her say she was in bed lying there with nothing on but her chemise. She thence jumped through the trap door into the cellar with Miss McCrea, and I will give you her very expression with regard to her being taken out of the cellar. Said she, "Big and heavy as my arse is, my hair was stout enough to sustain the weight"—meaning she was lifted out of the cellar literally by the hair of her head.

She said the Indians pricked her with their bayonets and pushed her with the butts of their muskets to get her up the hill faster. Arrived at the camp in her chemise, she sent word to her cousin General Fraser of her situation. He stirred around and searched up clothes for her among the women, and thus she was arrayed at last in proper plight to be introduced to him and the other officers and their ladies.[47]

Charlotte Leslie (b. circa 1780) was a black woman, a former slave, who had known Dinah McCrea, "John McCrea's black woman in the time of the Revolutionary War."

Charlotte Leslie:

When I first came to live with Judge Edward Savage [*of Salem*] we became acquainted and were slaves together in his family many years until my marriage and freedom. Then again, after she was emancipated by the state law, she preferred living with us to remaining at Judge Savage's for she felt herself more free and equal at our house than there. So she resided with us until her death some fifteen years ago. I have heard her tell of Jane's murder by the Indians, et cetera a great many times.

The brothers James, John, and Samuel McCrea when they came to this country—I know not where they came from—settled in Ballstown in the midst of the woods, and their sister Jane was their housekeeper. When they came there was no mill within thirty miles of them and they used to boil wheat until it was soft and then make it into cakes.

Who John McCrea married for his first wife I do not know. But she was a violent Whig. John, her husband, was neutral or on both sides by turns. Jane, his sister, was a violent Tory. Jane and Mistress McCrea used to quarrel about the war, and Dinah used to say she several times stepped in between them to separate them, so angry would they get with each other.

Jane was up to Fort Edward visiting when she was murdered. Her brother had sent up his wagon for her to ride home but her friends urged her not to go back among the rebels so she stayed. So Dinah used to say. I have no recollection of Dinah's saying that she was with Jane at this time but she used to tell that Jane and Mistress McNeil jumped into the cellar and when the Indians pulled up the trap door Mistress McNeil cried out to them "Friends! Friends!"

Jane had on a light chintz frock and under this a black, callamink [*calamanco—a type of glossy, worsted cloth*] petticoat—so Dinah used to say. When the body was found, the bottom of the chintz gown had been cut off by the Indians—about a third or fourth part of the dress had been cut off. The body was placed on a float in the river for the purpose of bringing it down to her brother's to be buried. But Mistress McCrea said she did not want it brought there—so they stopped some ways above and buried it on the shore of the river.[48]

The burial Dinah referred to must be the second one, when according to Robert Blake: "she was taken up and carried down to the Black House and reburied as I understood. This I suppose was done soon after Burgoyne's army left Fort Edward for Schuylerville."[49]

FLIGHT

The Allen and McCrea murders brought about the almost complete evacuation of Salem and Argyle. Tories and neutrals fled too because the danger from the Indians seemed just as great to them. (Both Allen and Jane McCrea had been Tory sympathizers.) This dramatic time in the war was the one people remembered best when they talked with Dr. Fitch years later.

Many of the New England settlers went back across the mountains to Massachusetts. The families of William Mc-Collister and Elizabeth Conkey Pratt were among this group.

William McCollister:

In Seventeen Hundred and Seventy-seven, when most of the families from around here fled, Father went with his family to Chesterfield in Massachusetts to his sister's, wife of Thomas Halbert. They left about the first of August and Father had a large field of wheat on the flat which he was obliged to leave unharvested. He had a span of horses. Mother rode one with the eldest boy behind her and the youngest child in her arms. Father rode the other, with the two other children on the horse with him. Judge Ebenezer Russell's wife accompanied them also on horseback with a babe in her arms. Judge Russell, himself, was thus enabled to remain at home. I think Judge Savage's wife also went with them but I am not certain. They crossed the kill down near More's bridge and went down through Pownal but the route beyond I do not know.

Father went and joined the army as soon as his family were safely landed at his sister's. He did not return here to harvest his wheat. He left the premises in charge of one Hunsdale and his wife, who were too old to undertake such a journey and said if they were killed here it would only shorten their lives but a few years.

It must have been late in the fall when the family returned for Hunsdale had got through with the butchering of the hogs. When mother became childish from old age, she was often talking of Chesterfield and this journey.[50]

Elizabeth Conkey Pratt:

Finally we all forsook our homes for a distant flight to our friends in New England. We had a large quantity of pewter dishes which we could not take and which would be stolen by the Tories unless they were concealed. Father dug a hole near the house and placed them all in it and his handsaw on top of them and covered them up.

The Tories at this time were greatly elated and carried their heads quite high but after Burgoyne's surrender and when we returned, they were greatly humbled and downcast.

I do not know which way our family fled or where we crossed the kill, but we went to Bennington and were there obliged to stay, Father's business as commissary to the militia rendering it impossible for him to go from Bennington for some time. Two of my uncles came up to Bennington from Pelham to take us down there. Eunice was an infant and Mary was sick with the measles, so that Mother had to remain and take care of her. We four older children went with our uncles. I remember nothing of the journey only its close—how we children forgot our fatigue and with light hearts ran up a long hill our uncles having told us "Grandpa's house" was at the top of it. Mother remained in Bennington till after the battle was fought there. After the battle, Father got released long enough to come with her to Pelham.[51]

The McMurray and Nelson families of Salem went south into Cambridge as Mrs. Martin and her children had done. John McMurray was the son of a Scotch-Irishman, Robert McMurray, who had arrived in Salem between 1774 and 1775.

61

John McMurray:

When the town was evacuated in Seventeen Hundred and Seventy-seven, I was an infant and was carried on my mother's back. Our goods were loaded on an ox-sled and the remainder of them buried. Father had many books, some of them that he valued highly. These were all buried and were quite spoiled when they were dug up again. We went south. Somewhere down in Cambridge we made a temporary stop of a day or two. Whilst there, Baum's detachment passed along south of us. It was at the house of a Mistress Miller that we tarried. As the troop of the enemy had passed, it was concluded to be folly to follow in their tracks and that we should be more safe at home. So we returned. Fields of wheat were everywhere standing and the women turned out to reap some in these. The weather was excessively hot and they were constrained to go almost naked. They therefore kept a sharp lookout to see if there was any men anywhere looking at them thus half-clothed, but none ever came in sight of them so entirely had the inhabitants moved off.[52]

Simon Nelson:

I was born opposite Stillwater on the east bank of the Hudson during the temporary sojourn of my family there [1765-1767] with the rest of the company who came over from North Ireland with Doctor Clark.

When the families fled from Salem in Seventeen Hundred and Seventy-seven Father had only a span of horses to aid in our flight. Mother and the youngest child rode one of these. Some of our goods and Samuel—who was sick at the time and but a small boy—was taken on the other. I believe there were no wagons in the town at this time. We went down to Sancoick close by the Dutch church. Froman or Vroman wanted Father and John Law to stay there and take charge of his place to allow him to fly to some more secure spot than that was for him, he being a committee-man and well-known. So they concluded to tarry there. He had commenced his haying and harvesting. We finished it. Suddenly word was

brought us that the British army was coming that way. About a dozen Salem families were there. I remember Alex Simpson; the Wilsons—Paddy and Joe, both old men then—McWhorter, Joe Cooper and William Tosh were all there at Sancoick with their families.

Everything was packed up in haste and we were ready to start the next morning, the army being encamped this night at Cambridge. But James More came along and told us all to lay still and quiet in the houses, for then we would not be molested, whereas if we were found moving off all we had would be taken from us. So we concluded to stay. But early next morning all the Salem horses, thirteen in number, were sent a mile down the river, my brother Joseph and others taking them to keep them away from the British. But as ill luck would have it, a man driving away cattle was pursued by a party of Indians and Tories from Cambridge that morning. They followed him south to the Walloomscoick River without succeeding in taking him. Then giving over the pursuit they followed up the river to join the army at Sancoick and came thus directly upon our horses and seized the whole of them. Father applied to Skene for ours but . . . [*not recollected*]. When the Indians passed back flying from Bennington Battle, I saw one of them riding by on one of our horses and wished with all my heart he would stumble and throw the Indian and escape from him.

Father and I went out in the morning to salt the sheep. Running to the top of the knoll and looking towards the house I saw Father entering it and the soldiers and the Indians all about the house and neighborhood like a swarm of bees. I had but one thought—to run and join Father. I first passed through a party of Indians having no fears of them, having been used to the Stockbridge Indians before this. They patted me on the head saying "Poor little boy – Bostonian boy." I got into the house in safety. The soldiers were plundering it of whatever they could find. One of them told Father to open the oven door, in which was an oven-full of bread just baked. Father did so, but one of the officers said "Will you take the bread away from these children?" So they let it remain.

On the day of the battle we were ever and anon receiving reports at Sancoick, first that the rebels were beat, then that the Tories were beat, then again that the rebels were getting the worst of it, and so it went first for one then for the other side.

Father and John Law happened to be among a party of Tories when they were all taken prisoner together. They were thus prevented from gathering any of the plunder of the battlefield in which work some of our neighbors were quite successful. They were confined three or four days when Doctor John Williams passing by asked, "What are you doing there in that company?" On informing him of their misfortune, they were speedily released. Neighbor Simpson was quite diligent in gathering plunder. He moved his goods from home on an ox-sled, but had three full loads to bring back—knapsacks, carts, wagons, et cetera.

When the discomfited British were retreating through Sancoick they destroyed all they could not take away. They knocked the hoops from a large quantity of flour in barrels. We durst not gather up any of this flour fearing poison had been scattered amongst it but the hogs fared sumptuously on it.

Immediately after the battle, Father and I came up home to look to our property. Found all safe and unmolested. But that night the hogs broke into our cornfield and we had much trouble in driving them out. Had we not come home as we did our corn crop would have been totally destroyed. A quantity of flour and, I believe, some clothing was sent by Gates' order, I suppose, to Salem to be distributed among those who had fled from their homes and thus lost their crops, which were just ripe as we went away. I know our family drew half a barrel of this flour which we received at Salem Village.[53]

Some of Salem's Scotch-Irish colony banded together to hide in the woods. Were they "Tories or neutrals" as Robert Blake says?

Sarah McCoy McNish:

In Burgoyne's time my father McCoy, David Tomb, William Moncrief, Daniel Mattison and some others fled together from their houses. Going down the north side of Battenkill we crossed it near James Campbell's and struck back from the kill into the woods where, hid from the world amid the hills on a dry spot partly in the midst of a marsh, we encamped for three weeks or more till the danger of the Indians destorying our houses became less menacing. We took our provision with us but drove down no cattle. Mattison and his wife went away from the others each evening to sleep in a separate place and some of them thought, although an old soldier, he was the most timorous man of the company. We had bowers erected covered with boughs of pine and hemlock in which we slept. I do not remember how we fared in rainy weather.

We were back home from there when the Battle of Bennington was fought, for I remember well of seeing my father McCoy standing up on a stump near our house and listening to the reports of the cannon in that direction. The sound was distinctly heard here in Salem, and it was at once known that it was an engagement with Baum's party, for we knew of this party having gone off in that direction.[54]

Robert Blake:

I know the spot well where the Salem folks herded their cattle in Jackson and encamped in Burgoyne's time. It was perhaps half a mile southwest of Alexander's house on the flat, back from the kill. They were Tories or at least neutrals and fearful their cattle would be seized to supply Mc-Cracken's company and other troops at Salem garrison. They drove them off down there to hide them. It was a secluded place entirely away from and out of sight of any of the roads where people passed at that time. They were there three or four weeks or more. Their families, if they went at all, did not stay as long as the cattle did. I always supposed it was the men only that were there to watch the cattle and that the women, children, et cetera remained at home. They probably crossed the kill at James Campbell's. Ere the dam was put up at Battenville, there was a very good fordway there at James Campbell's just below the island in the kill.[55]

Most of the Argyle people went to Burgoyne's camp, then at Fort Edward, to take "Protection." According to one old lady who talked to Dr. Fitch: "There were only two Whigs in the whole Argyle Patent in the Revolutionary War—Duncan Shaw and Ronald McDougall."[56]

Ann McArthur:

We knew nothing of the murder until the third night after. Uncle Alexander Campbell, who was then with the army as soon as it was ascertained that the scalps brought in by the Indians were those of the Allen family, became alarmed lest we were murdered also. He immediately started to see if we were safe—came to the Corners. Nobody there had heard anything about us, and he could get nobody to come with him to our house till passing Neal Gillespie's—who was reputedly a cowardly man but showed himself this time more courageous than his neighbors. Neal said he would go with him, for it would be too horrid for Uncle to come here alone and perhaps find us all murdered. So they came together

Sunday night when we were all asleep. They found the gate shut and the cattle all quiet in the yards and hence felt assured we were all safe. They came to the door and aroused us and told us of the murder and the alarm of the country west of us. It was considered that it was no longer safe for us to remain, as we left the house forthwith in the dead of night and went down to my Grandfather Campbell's ["*White*" *Duncan*] on the Duelly place, taking a direct pathway then running through the woods. I remember I was much gratified with this night's journey through the woods. The moon was very bright at the time. After staying two or three days at Grandfather's we returned home and a company gathered here to go into Burgoyne's camp.

We all felt safe and secure until the Allen murder. Allen was at our house, I believe, the day before the murder, making some arrangement with Father about shooting—that hearing the report of each other's guns they might know it was squirrels or other game they were shooting.

There was a crowd at our house the night we gathered to start for the camp and they were mostly women—scarcely any men among them. Where the men were, I don't know. Uncle Alexander, I know, kept a look out from a window in the chamber at the end of the house. Two other men stayed in a thicket of woods not far from the house for concealment. Doctor McDonald from Camden, I remember, was one that came here. He was very sick through the night and on his

67

account the children were stilled as much as possible. A small black girl belonging to Aunt Nancy Campbell was here and sitting on the floor. Her fingers were often stepped on but she was too terrified to cry out.

My grandfather had a considerable flock of sheep to drive over. His was the only wagon then in these parts. Some small children were carried over in it, though they had some difficulty in getting along, the road only being open for passengers on horseback. I know not whether the company that gathered at Esquire McNaughton's went over before or after us. I walked all the way over. I remember as we passed Allen's house, the cap of the murdered babe, made of calico, was found on a stump beside the house all glued together with the dried blood. We went from here to Fort Edward in a day and stopped at the Campbell house. My sister, six years old, was taken sick while we were at Fort Edward and died a few days after we got home.[57]

Caty Campbell, her brother William Campbell, Eunice Campbell Reid, and Robert Blake all travelled to Fort Edward in the same party which gathered at the McNaughton house in East Greenwich, then a part of the Argyle Patent. Their memories of the trip and the time at Burgoyne's camp are not identical. Without contradicting one another on important points, each eye-witness saw and remembered things rather differently.

Caty Campbell:

We went to Fort Edward in a company with others from our neighborhood. On our way I went into Allen's house with others of the company. The broken plates, knives and forks and meat from the table were scattered over the floor, which was all tracked with blood—the blood of the poor Negro who it appeared had fought bravely against the Indians. Everyone was screaming and crying when we came out of the house.

I remember when on our way, we came to a party of Indians who had killed a hog and hung it up to dress it. When they saw us they flew for their guns which they snatched up ready to attack us. But on seeing a British officer and his scout of men who were accompanying us for our protection, they fled into the woods and we saw no more of them.

At Fort Edward, I remember seeing Burgoyne talk with Father and shed tears. He was a thick-set man, not tall.

LIEUTENANT GENERAL BURGOYNE

Mother died while we were at Fort Edward—of jaundice—the tenth of August. The doctor gave her an emetic and she died under the operation of it. "White" Duncan Campbell's wife also died there.[58]

Caty's memory of Burgoyne shedding tears may not be as unlikely as it sounds. According to his biographer, Gerald Howson, the General was an unusually open, generous-spirited man. On more than one occasion after Saratoga, he "actually shed tears" when moved by the kindnesses of his captors.[59] Was General Burgoyne moved to tears by the plight of the "Argyle people"? It is an interesting thought.

William Campbell:

All the families from around here went in company together. My father and his family were the forward one in the train. I think we went from here there in one day, driving our cattle with us. I walked as did all who were able to do so. My mother rode on horseback, being in rather poor health.

The children too young to walk were secured on horses. When crossing the Fort Edward flats as we were approaching the house of one Lindsay, the first house on this side of Fort Edward and some two miles from there, a [Canadian] Indian was dressing a hog which he had killed. Seeing us approaching, he caught up his gun and was about shooting at Father, when a British officer came in sight behind him; whereupon he ran into the woods. Soon after this there was a cracking of musket shots out in the woods, perhaps half a mile from Lindsay's house, towards Fort Edward. A party of [Canadian] and of Stockbridge Indians had encountered each other in the woods, and out of our sight. The firing was heard at the post and a party of soldiers was sent out to aid their Indian allies. On their arrival the Stockbridge Indians gave over the fight and fled.

We stayed at Fort Edward a month, I should think, living in the house of a namesake of ours, Mistress Campbell, from which house Miss McCrea had been taken. The cows were yarded all together at night. By day they were turned out, but if they got into the woods or out of sight of the fort, they were liable to be killed by the Indians, or at least to be milked dry by the soldiers. So it was my daily employment whilst there, to watch or herd our cattle and keep them in sight of the camp. One day, I remember, a young Indian three or four years older than me came and commenced quarrelling with me, and finally began to cuff me. I hereupon whipped him with my goad so that he halloed out; when a great Indian ran to us, caught me as in a vice, drew his scalping knife, and shook and flourished it about my head. But a British officer now came and took my part, picked up a club and laid it over the back of the Indian, scolding him roundly, and told me to whip every Indian that abused me or attempted to molest me.[60]

Eunice Campbell Reid:

The country was greatly alarmed before the Allen murder. This increased it tenfold. It was an awful time—such as the present generation can have no conception of. No families

70

felt safe in remaining in their houses overnight. We at Roger Reid's forsook the house regularly every night for some time. At first we slept in the hay barrack but not deeming this a secure retreat, we withdrew into the thicket of hemlocks that grew a piece north of the house and there slept night after night.

Scouting parties were continually patrolling the country watching every movement and helping themselves to a meal of victuals whenever they wanted it and continually keeping us in fear. John Barnes led the Salem scout which frequently passed our house. Adams' scout was one of the most active and oftenest heard of. I think this was a British scout but am not certain where it belonged. [*Adams's scout was a Tory company based in Arlington, Vermont*] One Sabbath a scouting party came along, caught one of our sheep and butchered it. They came into the house with the mutton and called for whatever they needed for cooking it, dug some potatoes also, then placed their meal upon the table and ate what they wanted, leaving all that remained for our use. Thus they made free with the inhabitants, who had to submit to it passively.

It was in the evening that all the families gathered at Esquire McNaughton's to go into Burgoyne's camp. All the families along Battenkill and its vicinity were in the company. Deacon Thomas Collins from Salem was there and also his father-in-law's family—Thomas McCrea whose daughters besides Mistress Collins were Martha and Betsy—Archy Livingston, "Black" Duncan Campbell, William Blake, John Fos-

71

ter, Duncan Campbell, Senior, Archy Campbell. In short, all
the families around gathered there with their horses, cattle,
and sheep. The sheep were bleating constantly through the
whole night. Much of the stock never returned being sold to
the commissaries of Burgoyne's army or killed by the Hessians for beef whenever they could find a cow out of sight of
its owner or unguarded.

I do not remember about any alarm that night, but it
might have been so, and the youngerly men might have with-
drawn. We started early the next morning. The stock was all
drove in a herd together. I carried the whole distance a child
two or three years old—half-sister to Roger Campbell. It was
a most fatiguing lug. I think we went entirely through one
day. We went past Allen's house and took a resting spell there.
The moccasin tracks of the Indians were marked in blood all
over the floor; the dishes and knives were scattered about.
We also made a pause to rest ourselves at Yerry Killmore's
and another at Lindsay's house. At Lindsay's the floor was all
torn up by the Indians who had been there searching it for
plunder.

At Fort Edward we stayed at Esquire Campbell's house.
The house was full to overflowing with families that were there
for protection. We occupied part of the chamber, Archy Livingston another part. The two Duncan Campbells and Archy
Campbell were quartered in the lower story of the same house.
We were there a week or two—over one Sabbath, I know—
for it was said there was preaching in the camp just above us
on that day. I also remember a funeral of a lieutenant in the
army. The procession came down from the camp to the burying ground and at the close of the burial three volleys were
fired over the grave.

The Hessians or Brunswickers as they were called there
wore their beards on their upper lips parted each way, and
curled around the corners of their mouths.

Both the Duncan Campbells lost their wives there. Old
Duncan's wife died of dysentery. There was no medical attendance to be had. Black Duncan's wife was sick two or three
days, speechless all the time. I was going upstairs and found

her sitting halfway upstairs looking very unusually. I spoke to her but she made no reply. I ran and told Mistress Livingston that Mistress Campbell would not speak to me. She came and we soon found she could not speak. We got her onto a bed and I watched beside her, brushing off the flies, et cetera, till she died.

A little daughter of Archy Campbell's named Nancy also died there. Archy thought the air was so confined and impure in the crowded house she would do better if she could be in the fresh air. So he made out to get a tent and erected it near the house, and his family and the sick child moved into it—but the child died.[61]

Robert Blake:

A few days after the murder of the Allen family the families from around here gathered at Alexander McNaughton's house to go into Burgoyne's camp for protection. Their stock was all turned together into Esquire McNaughton's meadow, and the families were in and about his house overnight to start on our journey early the next morning. Captain Mc-Cracken, with his trained company of soldiers raised from around here, was then garrisoning Salem Fort—as the picketed church was called. I don't know how many men he had, but it was a strong company which he had raised some time before. The pickets were then recently placed around the church, the work having been several days in doing, folks turning out from all around to help them.

Some time in the night, whilst the families were gathered at Esquire McNaughton's, an alarm was given that Mc-Cracken's company was on its march to take us prisoners. All was consequently in the utmost terror and confusion, the women weeping and wailing and the men flying from the house, leaving their wives and children, knowing that Mc-Cracken's company would not injure them, but that the men would be taken and imprisoned if they were caught. The men withdrew in a body to fly to the camp. I was most anxious to accompany the men, but Father forbade me, saying I was so young—sixteen years old—that the assailants would do me no harm or wouldn't hurt me. So I had to stay. But in a very short time they sent back for me in haste. They wanted me for their guide, none of them being well enough acquainted with the road to travel it in the night without a risk of losing their way. Glad was I of this.

We hastened on and reached Yerry Killmore's by night, where they stayed overnight. They did not go through in one day, as William Campbell supposes. One Duncan Lindsay, as William Campbell supposes, lived in the first house this side of Fort Edward, full three miles from the fort. I remember nothing of the Indian skirmish of which he speaks but it probably was as he says. The next day early, I was sent back to guide and help the families and cattle along. I met them soon after they had started from Killmore's. On our way thence to Fort Edward, I remember well, we met a worthless vagabond, whose name I cannot now recall. He had belonged to

Captain McCracken's company and had deserted from it and joined Burgoyne. Six Indians accompanied him. He said they had started out to take the fort at New Perth and that we would soon meet a company of six hundred Indians that were on their way for this business. This frightened and appalled the women very much for they expected that their Salem acquaintances would all be murdered. But we met no Indian force and the intelligence was false, but at the moment it scared us excessively.

The fort at Fort Edward was put up in the Old French War, of logs, covered with an embankment of sand. The logs had decayed and the sand slid down when the Revolution commenced, so that only the corner towards the Widow Campbell house was occupied by the Americans when Miss McCrea was taken. It was some buildings in this corner of the fort from which they came out to fire upon the Indians; all other parts of the fort were dilapidated or nearly worthless. Burgoyne did not occupy the fort at all. His army encamped on the green around it and up near the hill in their tents, and the officers had their headquarters in the Doctor Smith house which was not picketed at that time. But in the following years of the war pickets were placed around the Doctor Smith house enclosing perhaps an acre of ground and here the garrison was quartered—the buildings in the corner of the old fort being then occupied only for workshops and baggage rooms.

I remember Colonel Philip Skene well and also his son Major Skene—these were the titles by which they were called in Burgoyne's camp. The Colonel was a large, portly, fine-looking man; his son was smaller and more slender. It was Colonel Skene that administered the oath of allegiance to all the inhabitants who flocked to Burgoyne's army and gave them certificates, under his own signature, of their having taken the oath and being therefore entitled to protection and permission to pass from the camp to their homes.

[My Uncle Bell's] house was about twenty rods from the main road. It was a log house with but one large room. Two or three rods east of it was a noble, large spring directly from which quite a brook ran. This spring was in great repute at the camp; the wash women and the men used to come to it, many of them, to wash their clothes.

Duncan Bell and I were employed daily to herd my uncle's and my father's cattle whilst I stayed there. My father drove over but one cow and a yoke of young steers, two or three years old. If they were not watched or got out of sight, there was danger of their being killed by the Indians. The cows all had bells on that rang much louder than the cowbells

75

of a later day. At night they were driven into my uncle's yard, and there were sentries standing there that rendered them safe. A provostmaster was stationed in my uncle's barn, having about twelve American prisoners under his charge in the barn, and a number of Hessians to guard them. The Indians painted the faces of these prisoners in a horrible manner. Some were painted entirely black with a bright red stripe across their necks in front, looking at first glance as though their throats were cut. Others had the black on their faces spotted and marked with red, like the lakes and rivers drawn upon a map. Probably this was intended to represent gashes in the face with the blood streaming from the wounds. They looked awful. A British officer happening in the barn asked why they did not wash the paint off. "I did not know as we had liberty to do so" replied one of the men. Water was immediately thereupon procured and the men gladly washed off the paint. These men were confined there till a day or two before we came home from Fort Edward.[62]

Before Saratoga

Caty Campbell:

While we were at Fort Edward, the Whigs tore down our fences and let the cattle into our grain fields, whereby it was nearly destroyed. Father had two horses which he took to Fort Edward and sold, receiving his pay in solid gold. We had four cows. Soon after we got back home, "Mad" More [*James More*] came with some men from Sodom, to drive off our cows. They threw down the fence and went to driving them out of the field, when Father got around them and drove them back. More then came up to him, and putting the muzzle of his loaded gun to Father's breast said "Stand still, you d--d Tory or I'll shoot you through!" And the other men then drove the cattle away, while More kept Father away from them. They took them to Sodom and cast lots for them. One of them fell to Bill Smith who, the next day, drove her back home to us saying he could not take the milk from motherless children.

More foddered the cows that winter at a stack on the Sodom side of the kill, he living on the opposite side of the stream. At length on the breaking up of winter, high water came running over the top of the ice so that More could not cross it one day to feed the cattle. Towards night the cattle becoming hungry started off upon the path to the house and going on the ice to where the water was running, trying to wade across it, the ice had become so rotten they all fell in and were drowned—the three cows he had stolen from Father, and one of his own, and also a yoke of oxen he had stolen from somebody else.[63]

Mary Gillespie Bain:

When my father returned home with his family from Burgoyne's camp, he found three fine horses which had been kept in the pasture at home being dead and enormously swollen. They had been killed but a few days before, it was evident. We supposed the Indians had tried to catch them to steal them but not being able to catch them had maliciously shot them.

A day or two after my return, when we were all at dinner, five or six great Canadian Indians, their faces hideously painted making them look like very demons, came boldly into the door. We all fled from the table, we children affrighted, screaming "Mama, will they kill us?"—the murder of our neighbor Allen and his children being fresh in our minds. They, without any ceremony, sat down at the table and ate everything that was upon it. A pewter mug holding exactly a quart was on the table filled with milk. An Indian took it up and drank the whole at a draught. Another took the mug, went to the milk pan, dipped it up full and drank it off. Another followed his example, then another and when the last of the milk was poured into the mug, my mother ventured to step up to the Indian and with a look pointed to us children and then to the mug and thus made him understand that we needed the milk more than he did. He thereupon set down the mug.

Having consumed all our eatables, they went out. My father showed them the dead horses and by his motions gave them to understand that Indians had killed them. They looked around and examined the horses very sagely and then shook their heads and made motions to Father to explain to him that it was not Indians' work, but that they had been killed in some other way. But he knew better and insisted upon it to them that it was Indians.

From our house they went south one and one-half miles to old Archy McNeil's. They plundered his house, he and the family not having yet returned from the camp. At length the Indians came back to our house, the same afternoon, each with a great pouch as heavy as he could carry. One of them came up behind Mother and patted her on her left arm, which was bare, with something hard. She supposed it was his tomahawk. She durst not show any resentment but remained perfectly passive. The Indian thereupon struck her arm so hard

78

that she turned her head enough to perceive that it was not his tomahawk but a woman's shoe that was in his hand. He placed the shoe in her hand with a motion from which she knew he intended she should take it as a present from him. She motioned to him that a single shoe was of no value, two being necessary. He put his hand into his bosom and drew out the mate to it and handed [it] to her.

The next day Mister McNeil and family returned from the camp and stopped at our house to rest on their way. My mother brought the shoes and gave them to her [*Mrs. McNeil*]

"Where did you find them?" she asked. "An Indian gave them to me yesterday" my mother replied. At once she cried out "Oh, we are ruined!"[64]

Eunice Campbell Reid:

When on our way home from Burgoyne's camp we stopped several days at John McNeil's. Whilst there a large party of the Brunswickers, to the number of thirty or more, came and went into Mister McNeil's potato field and dug a considerable part of the crop. Each of them had three knapsacks or bags which they filled with potatoes and carried off, one knapsack on the back of each and a bag or knapsack under each arm. Two of them had but one knapsack each but they took some pairs of tow-cloth trousers that were hanging out to dry, tied up the bottoms of the legs then filled them with potatoes, tied them up, and taking one under each arm went off with the trousers as well as their contents.[65]

Susan Lyttle Vance:

When we moved [*in the evacuation*] we had but one horse. A fine yoke of oxen was Father's main team at that time, and these oxen had been stolen from them and driven away to

Burgoyne's camp by two Salem Tories, John Todd and John Cloughlin. They offered Father a receipt for the oxen by which he might get his pay they said, but he would not take their receipt.

We went on foot down into Cambridge and stayed at McCool's, who lived near Wait's Corners. Of the Salem families many stopped around there; others went on to Bennington and down into Massachusetts. On Sabbath, Doctor Clark had the folks all gathered together for divine service. The meeting was on a rise of ground above the Owlkill—the outlet of the Jackson ponds [*which*] ran into the valley below. I don't remember how long we stayed at McCool's. Father came back first to see about saving his grain, and he was taken sick and sent Mother word—for folks were passing through the country all the time—and so she went back home with me and Jane and Rebecca.

Rebecca and I went out after dinner to pull flax, alone, not far from the house. A Hessian soldier with his gun and military clothes came along, enquiring in broken English the way to Bennington. He was deserting from the British [*at Fort Edward*] and finding his way through the country to New England. But he told us he was in advance finding the road to Bennington, and that the whole army was not far behind him. This so alarmed Rebecca that eager to get all the news from him we could we followed him—conversing with him—many rods, till we got to the foot of the hill south of our house. Suddenly we heard a crackling among the bushes. A party of Tories were secreted on the little hill east of the road, at the foot of the big hill. Who they were I do not know. There was more than a dozen of them. They rushed upon the Hessian, took away his gun, pinioned him and said they should take him back to the camp to be shot for deserting. They also said we girls had got to go with them, too, for we we traitors showing a deserter the road for him to escape.

They also captured on the road Judge Hopkins of Rupert, a well-known Whig. They marched us along the road past our house, which stood away from the track we followed, and we got out nearly to where David Russell now resides when we were met by William McNish who was a frank Tory now coming from Burgoyne's camp, and knew the party that was taking us away. He asked what they were doing with us little girls. They told him they were taking us to Fort Edward for aiding a deserter to escape. He told them they would not do any such thing—that our mother would go crazy if we were missed and would think we had been killed by the Indians. On his promising to keep us till after sundown, they gave us over into his care—their only design probably being to prevent our going home and telling of their taking off the Hessian till after they could get beyond the reach of a pursuing party which they probably feared would be rallied and sent after them. McNish accompanied us back home and stayed to watch us till dark, when he went on home over the hills.

My two brothers Isaac and William were working some land at West Hebron. From this place they were taken prisoners by a party of Tories, and carried to the British camp at Fort Edward where William was attacked by the measles. From hence they were taken down to Ticonderoga where they were confined with many other prisoneers. But the Americans attacked and captured the buildings in which they were confined and set them free [*September 18, 1777*]. The magazines were broken into and boxes of valuables were thrown open and every man told to help himself, to take what he could find by way of remuneration for what they had suffered. A chest was opened and everyone was thrusting in his hands and drawing out for himself. Brother William was too sick to share in this plunder and Isaac went up to the chest and drew out a small neat bible and a pair of silk stockings, and desisted from taking more. The next man thrust his hand in and drew out a heavy bag, but whether of gold or silver or what it was, they only could judge from the external appearances, for there was no time to pause and examine.

My brothers were released, and contrived to drag themselves over the hills and mountains down to Skenesborough. Thence they sent word home. And Charles Hutchison, our kind neighbor, mounted his horse and rode up to Skenesborough and brought them home, William before and Isaac behind him—William being so feeble he had to support him in his arms the whole distance. A large abscess had formed in his side, so large that Doctor Clark would not venture to open it fearing he might die immediately on the operation. So he could only recommend him to the kind mercy of God. At length the abscess broke and after discharging some time it spontaneously healed.

It was one of the Gillis' of Argyle that came over to Salem to tell us that William was sick with the measles at Fort Edward. Mother was so anxious for him that she determined to go to the British camp to find him and take care of him. She went over on foot to Fort Edward and, finding he was not there, she followed on after the army that was now moving down the river. She overtook the army and was in the camp one night—the night after "The Friday Battle" as it was called [*First Battle of Bemis Heights*]. The scene that she encountered that night beggars description. All was confusion, running to and fro, the blood flowing from the wounded as they were brought into the hospital, and the groans of the dying being everywhere heard. All were too busy and anxious to notice her or listen to her errand. But she met with a young man who came from the same county in Ireland she came from and who knew some of her relatives and old acquaintances there; and he interested himself in her behalf. She found that William was not there, nor could she gain any intelligence respecting him. Unable to endure another night of such horrors, she next day stole away from the camp with a blanket over her head and wrapped around her, hoping if anyone observed her that they would deem her a squaw wandering about. The river was covered with battoes, passing up and down. She reached Schuylerville, and when all was still, late in the night, she waded across the river at Deridders ferry and next day travelled sixteen miles, reaching William Reid's at Fitch's Point, where once more among friends and acquaintances she gladly tarried over night.[66]

Isabel Duncan McIntyre:

All day long we at Munro's Meadows heard the sound of the cannon at the battle of Saratoga although it was thirty miles away. My mother was confined and my youngest sister was born upon that day.[67]

1778 AND 1779

After Burgoyne's surrender in October 1777, Washington County had a kind of breathing space before a new wave of trouble in 1780. The British made several big raids against frontier settlements west of the Hudson in the years 1778 and 1779, but for this county it was only a time of constant "alarms" and perhaps some small-scale raids. Local loyalists and neutrals had a very hard time during these years.

Caty Campbell:

A school house stood at the top of the hill above the Widow McDougall's, by the side of the road as it ran at that time. The spring after Burgoyne's surrender the house was burnt, set on fire in the night by the Whigs, it was not doubted. The children's books, among which it was said there were [many] Bibles, burnt in the school house. This burning the word of God was much talked about among the Argyle Tories in the neighborhood and town.

A few nights after the school house burnt, my father's house was also burnt. It was a log house standing near the Battenkill at the head of the valley, below the Widow Dougall's. Father was at that time making sugar from trees of Archy Campbell's, on the opposite side of the kill a mile or nearly so below our house and wholly out of sight of it. He used to stay at the sugar camp over night to keep the fires under the kettles, leaving us small children all alone in the house, but coming by day home to see us and get his provisions. That night however, a presentiment came to his mind that he must go home, though he had no particular thought of any danger. He came, crossed the kill in his boat, and got to the house just in time to snatch us children out of our beds and carry us outdoors. Nothing else in the house was saved, though we had no furniture of any great value. That the house had been set on fire was certain, for it was the opposite end

84

of the house from the fireplace that was all on fire when Father first came in sight of it.[68]

Jacob Bitely:

In Seventeen Hundred and Seventy-eight Father left his place in Vermont—it was so risky living there, and we moved to Whitehall where we remained one year. One Burroughs, a Yankee, had evacuated his house there when Burgoyne came down, and was staying down in Salem or somewhere thereabouts. We moved into his house and tilled his land, raising a field of corn. In the fall he came up and wanted half the produce of the farm, and Father gave it to him.

When we were living in Whitehall, Skene's forge was standing on the west side of Wood Creek opposite his house. This was built of stone, a medium-sized building, square, about as large each way as his house was wide. There had been one or more sawmills at the falls but these were down. I think there was no gristmill or I should have seen the stones laying about somewhere. Skene seemed to have made the reducing of iron ore his chief business. We had to go over to Poultney River for our grinding, where there was a small gristmill with one run of stones, and so overrun with work, we often had to stay overnight to get our grist ground.

On the same side of Wood Creek were a few shanties or small buildings, botched up by our men for baking bread for the American army, and only temporarily occupied for this and similar purposes. I well remember, I, with other boys there, used to try to look into the room where Skene had kept his wife unburied. It was in the cellar of his stone house; a small apartment was walled up in one corner. This had a door leading into it and in the door was a single pane of glass. It was said that to draw an annuity left to his wife, he placed her corpse in this room, and yearly used to make out the papers, then go into this room, place a pen in the fingers of the corpse and guide the fingers to make the necessary signature to the writings, then forward the papers to England and draw the money upon them. The corpse was found in this room when the Americans took the place, and she was taken out and buried. The outer door of the cellar was left open and the door to this vault was closed. We boys used to go in at the outer door, cautiously and silently advance to the door of the vault, raise up on our tiptoes, peek through this pane of glass—all was dark within so that nothing could be distinguished there—then fearing a ghost would appear among us we would scud out of the cellar like scared sheep.

But although the land about Whitehall suited Father well enough, he did not feel that we were safe and secure in making a purchase there. We should be better guarded, he said, to be in the rear of Fort Edward. So he came down here, and bought out a rank Tory, on the opposite side of the river named Tuttle, father of John and William Tuttle, and here we moved in the spring of Seventeen Hundred and Seventy-nine. Our farm lay on Snoot Kill , and our house stood south of the mouth of Snoot Kill . The farm was all cleared up and under cultivation. Other Tories about there also sold out and went to Canada about the same time with Tuttle; for they began now to despair of the King's conquering this country; and the Whigs were getting to feel in such high spirits, they could not bear to remain in the neighborhood. The Widow Jones and her sons sold their place to Philander Doty; Malloy, George Campbell and another Campbell, all Tories on the opposite side of the river, sold out about this time, as did some others there of less note.

The defense of this frontier in Seventeen Hundred and Seventy-nine and Seventeen Hundred and Eighty and probably longer was entrusted to Colonel Warner's Vermont regiment. Captain Bronson's company was stationed at Fort George, Captain Chipman's at Fort Edward—it contained about forty men, I should think—and there were two companies, I believe, at Schuylerville. The woods between Glens Falls and Fort George were the most dark, doleful, and dangerous I ever saw. Father and I passed through them in Seventeen Hundred and Seventy-nine. Having some butter to spare, we took it up there and disposed of it to the garrison, taking salt for pay, which was then difficult to be got and far more valuable than the Continental money. On the way an enemy might anywheres have darted upon us out of the thick woods and murdered us without any chance for our escape.[69]

1780

"The winter of 1780" is the winter of 1779—1780.

Donald McDonald:

Just before I went to reside with Captain John Armstrong in Salem in the year Seventeen Hundred and Eighty, a namesake of his came from Canada with a supply of goods and opened a store in Captain John's house. This Armstrong, I believe, was no connection to Captain John. He was a little fellow, so small that at a rod or two distant anyone would have taken him to be a boy. He was born in Ireland, where he had been raised for a jockey to ride horses at races, and was the most expert rider I ever knew. To accommodate Little Armstrong, Captain John's family moved from the frame house into a smaller log house that stood in back of it, and Little John occupied the frame house with goods. He married that winter. All the Armstrongs went to the wedding, which was at Londonderry in Vermont. This wedding had taken place just before I went to live at Captain Armstrong's.

Little Armstrong had got one Bininger to come and tend store for him. Little Armstrong, having come from Canada to Salem, could not be regarded as a Tory, for a Tory never would have done such a thing. But Bininger belonged to the town, and had gone thence to Canada, and had now come back after being in Canada a few years. He must have been thirty years old, I should think. Little Armstrong had got Bininger to sell out the rest of his goods, Armstrong himself having left, I think, without intending to live any longer in Salem.

One evening that winter, a party of Whigs came to drive Bininger out of town. Among them were Bob Conkey, the McCrackens—David and John—from up White Creek, and from the west part of town, McCoy, Pennel, the Carswells, and others—six or eight sleigh-loads in all. They stopped a piece from the house, and Conkey went into the house disguised and asked if a store was kept there. He said he wanted to buy some goods. They told him the clerk had gone to bed upstairs. He went upstairs and told Bininger to get up and come down. But Bininger was reluctant to do so. Now one or two others came up the stairs; they stripped down the cloths and struck him two or three times with their whips. Finding he was in their power, he got up and went down. They took him into the sleighs and drove off post haste into Vermont, where they tied him to a tree, it was said, and all passing around him, each struck him a blow with their whips. They then unbound him and he left the place. Whether he came back to Salem, I don't know, but he certainly was not seen there for a long time.

Captain John was exasperated at this act and made a song about it, which he sang on town meeting day to a crowd, telling of the cowardice of the party: so many coming in the night to take off a single man. David Carswell had heard of Captain John's having this song and had himself made, or got one made, in answer to it which he stepped out and sang at the close of Captain John's singing, containing some slurs upon the Armstrongs and their friends. This touched Samuel McCarter who, when Carswell had ended his song, stripped off his coat and said if anyone there had anything against the Armstrongs or McCarters, let him come and try titles as to their courage. Thus challenged, David Carswell stripped off his coat. A ring was formed and at it they went. McCarter appeared to be getting the upper hands of Carswell, when Captain John swore he would lick the first man that at-

tempted to interfere—they should have a chance to fight it out fairly. No one dared interefere, and McCarter got the better of Carswell in the contest.

I cannot remember a verse of either of the songs. The crowd that stood around when they were being sung to laughed heartily; part on one side and part on the other.[70]

John McMurray:

I only remember the opening stanza of the Whig song. The turnpike above the village was settled all along by Doctor Clark's people, and was therefore always called Monaghan Street in those times, from these Monaghan Irish.

The song began thus: "Twas past eight o'clock as the watch did divide—Up Monaghan Street eight of us did ride . . ."[71]

Donald McDonald recalled another brawl among the excitable Salem Whigs. This probably dates from 1779 or after: "On one occasion More and Lyttle had a fight. A man named Robinson was arrested as a suspected person and tried before the Committee of Safety, which met at the house of Doctor Williams. More was present and was so abusive to Robinson that Lyttle, who was a good Whig, interfered; whereupon More turned his abuse upon Lyttle calling him a Tory. This made Lyttle's blood boil. He knocked More down and kicked him repeatedly, bestowing lavishly upon him his wonted exclamation when in anger: 'You d--d son of a whore.' "[72]

In March of 1780, the British sent a relatively small raiding party against Skenesborough—small compared with the big raid of the coming October. Andrew Skene, the slender youth Robert Blake remembered seeing at Fort Edward, was one of the loyalist officers leading the attack.

Deacon Cook's sister:

When Skenesborough was captured by the Indians, I well remember all the families along Granville River, from its mouth up to Father's on the edge of Pawlet, fled from their dwellings to our house and stayed there a week or two ere they dared venture to return to their homes. Father's was the lowest family on the river that did not forsake their house. McCall, who was murdered by the Indians, kept several cows and sold milk to the garrison. He and his wife were killed, and it was reported the Indians also killed all his cattle—ripping them open and carrying off their unborn calves.[73]

James Rogers:

I was born at Londonderry in New Hampshire, April Twenty-first, Seventeen Hundred and Sixty-three. My father, James Rogers, was a sucking infant when he was brought in his mother's arms from 'Derry in Ireland. When I was two years old, my father moved to Bashenringe [*Basking Ridge*] in New Jersey, and when I was twelve years old he moved to Salem, New York and settled on a farm in Blind Deer Hollow.

In Seventeen Hundred and Seventy-nine, I was in service nine months, stationed most of the time at Whitehall. I went as a substitue for another man who had been drafted, one Billy Pogue who lived in the south part of the town. I served his nine months out and received his wages. In Seventeen Hundred and Eighty, I was captured at Whitehall and kept prisoner in Canada till Seventeen Hundred and Eighty-two as told below.

In Seventeen Hundred and Eighty, Whitehall was the most advanced post occupied by the Americans, Ticonderoga and Crown Point being in ruins. All the settlers along Lake Champlain, too, had evacuated their homes. Whitehall was garrisoned by drafts from the militia of Salem and Cambridge. In March, Seventeen Hundred and Eighty, I was one of sixty men that were drafted to serve for a fortnight.

We were quartered at Skene's house. This house was of stone, some thirty feet by forty in size, two stories high and with windows in the roof. Skene's stone barn stood some distance this side of the house, and there was a third building for a storehouse. These three were all the structures then standing at Whitehall. Skene had ironworks, a gristmill, a sawmill, and probably houses or huts for the workmen, but all these had been destroyed at this time. A path led off east towards Vermont along the south side of the mountain; on this path at a distance of three-quarters of a mile from Skene's house stood a log house in which a man named McCall and his wife lived. She was the washerwoman for the troops. He was an old British soldier who had served in the French War.

Our fortnight expired and the party that was to come to take our places did not arrive. Our provisions were almost all consumed. As the ice on the lake was now breaking up, it was thought there was no danger just at this time of any of the enemy coming up from Canada to molest us, and it would therefore be safe for most of the men to return home and leave only a guard behind. So a company of twelve men was selected. I was one of this twelve.

On the morning of March Twenty-first, our comrades left us—they expecting to reach their homes in Cambridge and Salem before night. As my clothes by this time had become badly soiled and dirty, I set out to take them to the washerwoman's, Missus McCall. On reaching their home, found them absent—they having started to bring some washed clothes to the soldiers. Returning, when I was onto the main road, I saw McCall and his wife ahead of me. They were near Skene's barn and I some rods behind them, when hearing a rustling in the woods and bushes beside me, I saw two Indians coming out of them towards me. I was unarmed, so I took to my heels, and one of the Indians after me. I saw he was gaining on me—I was then a boy but sixteen years old—when he halloed to me in good English to stop and he wouldn't hurt me. I promptly stopped. He told me that I must go with him to Montreal.

As McCall and his wife were passing Skene's barn, a party of Indians came out of it to take them. McCall had a staff in his hand. I saw him strike at an Indian with this. Immediately thereupon, both he and his wife were stabbed with a sergeant's spontoon, a kind of spear which the Indian had, and fell dead upon the spot. Their bodies were dragged away into the bushes.

At the same time, the men at Skene's house were attacked. The party of the enemy consisted of one hundred and thirty Canadian Indians, two Canadian Frenchmen for their officers, and a Tory refugee who served as their guide in leading them to the spot. Our men concluded it would be their only chance to escape to rush to the creek and cross it in a battoe moored there. Alas, on reaching the battoe they found it had been drawn onto the land—by some of themselves who had forgotten this circumstance. They took to the water of the flooded and ice-cold stream, but ere they had any of them got across, the Indians reached the shore and ordered them to swim back or they would shoot every man. So they returned and surrendered themselves as prisoners.

We were now started for Canada. When we reached the summit of Whitehall Mountain, all four of the buildings— Skene's house, barn, the rough-boarded store house, and the farm dwelling half a mile south—were in flames below us, and not a roof remained where the village of Whitehall stands.

We went about three or four miles the first day, encamping for the night across East Bay in the present state of Vermont. We, the second day, proceeded by land nearly down to Ticonderoga and there went upon the ice of the lake, which was still firm all the way to Canada. Thus we kept on until, at length, we reached Saint John's. From here we were taken by the Indians to their villages, west, at Chateaugee [*Chateaugay*] and French Mills. My clothes were old and poor and were therefore not meddled with by the Indians. But whoever had a good coat or vest, it was taken from him.

In about a week most of us were taken to Montreal and sold to the British authorities at a joe—eight dollars—a piece. We now went separately before Colonel Campbell for examination. This Colonel Campbell was a son of Duncan Campbell who lived in Argyle. The object of this examination was to tamper with us and induce us to enlist into the British service, and also to gather what information they could, respecting the state of the country.

When I was before him, he inquired all the most minute particulars, the price of provisions, et cetera. Salt was very scarce at this time as the British held New York. None was to be had except what was imported into Boston and brought thence overland to Albany. He inquired the price of liquor. I told him that in the course of the past winter I had known three dollars to be given for a gill of whiskey, and he chuckled at this indication of the straits to which the country was reduced. But when I told him that I had also known a gill of whiskey to be given for a silver sixpence, he readily understood that in the former instance pay had been made in continental money.

FORT AT CHAMBLY.

The company that I was taken with was divided between Montreal and Chambly and two or three of them remained with the Indians at Chateaugee. About thirty prisoners were in the Chambly prison, closely confined and fettered as closely that I could only move my feet the length of my great toe at a step. Our provisions were execrable and our allowance scanty. In the fall of Seventeen Hundred and Eighty-one, only seven vessels succeeded in getting into Quebec. The country was therefore in great straits for provisions. Some of the cattle that died of starvation and disease were ate, and horses were slaughtered for the soldiers and prisoners. Horse beef was our main diet for some time. This close confinement and bad fare wore greatly upon my health until I, at length, became so weak that I was taken out and sent to Montreal Hospital. After being in the hopsital a while, I was moved to Montreal Jail.

Several of our prisoners had enlisted into the British service. Two of these, Hugh Pennel of Salem and John Garter—

where Garter was from I don't remember—and possibly others were among the guard of Montreal Jail. With this influence in the guard, the prisoners succeeded in inducing the whole guard to join them in an attempt to escape from Canada. John Simpson, also of Salem, was one of the foremost of the prisoners in concerting this scheme. Arms and provisions were procured for supplying the whole of them well, the prisoners giving the guard their last farthing to buy provisons, et cetera, for their journey. The night was approaching, when John Simpson seeing a stranger among the guard, beckoned to him and communicated the whole plot.

The guards were flogged most severely. I saw their backs just after and it was the worst sight I ever saw—their backs were torn as though a pack of hungry dogs had gnawed and mangled them. The whole were then banished to Cote du Lac Island. John Simpson never returned home after this.

Sometime about September, Seventeen Hundred and Eighty-one, a merchant of Montreal, being in want of a young man to help him, applied to the general to allow him to take one of the prisoners into his family and I was selected. I now fared very well. The merchant's name was John Gabriel Beak, a Dutchman who before the war had been in business in Boston and there married a Yankee wife. I remained with him until I was exchanged and set at liberty June Tenth, Seventeen Hundred and Eighty-two. About sixty of us were released at this time. We were brought in the British shipping to Crown Point and thence in battoe to Whitehall, where we bade our British attendants good-bye and came home.[74]

Jacob Bitely:

In the summer of Seventeen Hundred and Eighty a party of men, and one or two women with them, belonging to the garrison at Fort George, took a battoe and went onto one of the islands down the lake to gather huckleberries, fish, et cetera. The huckleberries were very thick on the island and gathering them was their chief errand.

At night they drew the battoe on shore, turned it up sideways and built a fire beside it—the battoe warding off the wind—and lay down to sleep. The light could be, of course, seen a great distance, and attracted thither a party of Indians in their canoes. They found all sound asleep. With their guns, tomahawks, and knives they probably at the same moment of time dispatched the whole company, took off their scalps and made off with themselves, leaving the bodies strewed around the campfire.

Morning comes and one of the group begins to have a return of consciousness. The midsummer sun is pouring down its hot rays upon his naked skull. Unable to stand, he contrives to crawl within reach of some bread. This he soaks in the water of the lake at his side and then covers his aching head with it. The sentries at the fort heard the sound of the firearms, and in the morning a boat was dispatched to ascertain the cause. They approach the island and find the scalpless man sitting erect amid his slain companions.

The surgeon of Warner's regiment, Doctor Washburn, was stationed at Fort Edward and hither the revived man was sent for medical attendance. When he had so far recovered as to be able to walk, he asked permission to go out among the inhabitants where he could obtain milk and better nourishment than the stores of the garrison furnished. Leave was granted, and Father, being at the fort, invited him to come to our house for a few days. He came and was with us three or four days—all the top of his head enveloped in a plaster. He went back to the fort to have it dressed by the surgeon—then he went out for a few days to another family. Thus he passed the time till he recovered. What afterwards became of him I know not.[75]

———

In October of 1780, Major Carleton sailed south, "up" Lake Champlain, with a fleet of eight large ships and twenty-six flat-bottomed boats carrying about a thousand men—British, Indians, and Tories. One part of the force went east to raid settlements in northern Vermont. The larger part of the ex-

pedition, under Carleton himself, struck Forts Ann and George (October 10 and 11) burning them and capturing their garrisons. The raiders also burned the Hudson River settlements as far south as Sandy Hill—perhaps down to Fort Miller (according to Bitely).

Jacob Bitely:

The year Seventeen Hundred and Eighty has always been designated in this quarter as the year of the Great Burning, to distinguish it from the lesser burnings of separate buildings that occurred in other years. The Tories, as already stated, had mostly sold out their farms around here and moved off to Canada. But such was their feelings of hatred and spite and malevolence towards the Whigs, that it added gall to their feelings to remember that these were living in comfort in their old homes. A large company of Tory refugees volunteered, it would seem, to come down from Canada in company with Carleton's force and burn our houses. The Tuttles and George Campbell, it was always said and believed, were the leaders of this company.

It was a clear cold night sometime in October that they fell upon us and burned every house and barn on the west side of the river from Sandy Hill to Fort Miller. This took place the same time that Carleton came down and took Fort Ann and Fort George. Carleton stopped overnight in Kingsbury. The afternoon sun might have been an hour high when we saw the smoke of the houses they were burning in Kingsbury. At the same time, we saw the people rushing down the road on the east side of the river, men, women and children. Some of the folks crossed over to tell us that all Kingsbury was in flames and that all the folks on the east side of the river were flying from their homes. We could scarcely believe the enemy would have the audacity to cross the river and come directly in rear of the fort and burn our buildings and our neighbors' under the very guns of the fort. Still, we deemed it safest to fly.

My two oldest brothers were not at home at this time. They were enlisted in the American service and were sta-

97

tioned out in the west part of Saratoga County, at Palmerston, where a garrison was kept up to prevent marauding parties from Canada from coming down by the Sacendaga route and falling upon the inhabitants in the neighborhood of Ballston. We had two horses. We tied up our beds and most valuable and necessary clothing and tied them onto the horses backs. We then went up the river to the fort, three-fourths of a mile above the house, and there crossed to this, the east side—Father, Mother, my brother and myself. I well remember that I expected we should be fired upon and killed ere we got across the river. We then went down the river, travelling all night, and got to Winnie's, near Deridders opposite Schuylerville, at sunrise the next morning. Father still supposed it was not probable our house was burned, so he took one of the horses and rode directly back, but on coming in sight he at once perceived all our buildings were in ashes, and all our grain and hay was consumed. They also killed all our cattle and hogs.

Our house being burned, we hired a place near Deridder's and lived there through the year Seventeen Hundred and Eighty-one. We hired of one Winnie, a relation of Walter Deridder's and close by him. One Sheldon then occupied the lands on the south side of the mouth of the kill, and above him up the kill was Gerrit Springer, George Reynolds, and Rogers'. James Rogers' farm was on the north side of Battenkill at its mouth. All these families were Whigs.[76]

George Fowler and Austin Wells were in the same party of militiamen who went up to Fort George after the British raid in October 1780. Austin Wells' statement is probably more accurate about specific details: the number of bodies found, etc. But the younger George Fowler gives a more personal account in some ways: he lets us know his feelings as well as what he saw.

George Fowler was born in 1761 in South Kingston, Rhode Island. He moved to Cambridge, New York in 1770 with his father and other family members.

George Fowler:

In this county, when we came here in the spring of Seventeen Hundred and Seventy-eight, all the men between the ages of sixteen and forty-five were regularly enrolled in companies of militia and frequently assembled for training and drilling. There were few regulars, not more than fifty, stationed at Fort Edward, and to keep the fort garrisoned, men were drafted from the militia companies around to go to Fort Edward and serve there one month.

Thus the garrison was kept up through the season without the service coming very hard on any of us. I was drafted sometime in the summer and served nine months time. We had little to do. A file of three men was sent every day up to Fort George to see that all was right up there in the little garrison. I was sent up two or three times during the month I was out.

This was more risky service than any I had to do in Rhode Island, where the land was all cleared and we could espy an enemy at a distance. But from Glens Falls to Fort George, it was all woods and an enemy might at any moment start out from behind the trees along the road and be upon us without a moment's warning.

[*In October 1780 when the British raided Forts Ann and George.*] the Cambridge and the Hoosic companies were forthwith mustered. We marched on the usual route which led from Doctor Bullious' church past where Union Village [*Greenwich*] now is—though we did not ford the kill there—and on to Deridder's, thence up the river, fording Battenkill perhaps a half mile above its mouth. We reached Fort Edward at the close of the first day, encamping outside of the fort. The commanding officer wanted to take charge of us, at least in some measure, but our officers preferred acting entirely distinct and independent of him.

The next morning we were all paraded, some three hundred in number, and marched up to Glens Falls. A body of the Indians had penetrated down towards Schuylerville and burned some barracks down that way which were filled with wheat. They had crossed the river about Glens Falls in making this marauding incursion. We marched on up to Fort George which had been burned by the enemy who had just gone down the lake. The beams and other timbers of the fort were still smoking and burning when we arrived. The bodies of twelve men were found lying where they fell—scalped and shockingly mangled, bloated and black with partial mortification. It was a most horrid sight, on looking at which I turned faint and sick and had to turn away and lay down in the shade of a tree to recover. I could not aid in burying them. A hole was dug beside them, not very deep, in which they were all placed together and covered up.

We now started on our return and encamped that night part of the way back to Glens Falls. The next day, the third of our being out, we came back to Fort Edward and on half way or thereabouts to Fort Miller, occupying an old deserted log house around which was a patch of potatoes. We dug some of these, roasted and ate them, for we were most of us quite destitute of provisions. In good season, the next or fourth day, we reached Cambridge and were disbanded.[77]

Austin Wells:

I was born February Fourteenth, Seventeen Hundred and Fifty-nine and will soon be ninety years old. I came here [Cambridge] with Father on horseback in Seventeen Hundred and Seventy-three to visit Brother Edmund who had then settled here, and I stayed over the winter and then went back to Hebron [*Connecticut*]. I came up here again after my mother's death in February, Seventeen Hundred and Seventy-six, and this has been my residence ever since. In April Seventeen Hundred and Seventy-six I enlisted for one year— which was the custom in the early part of the war, short enlistments—and was stationed up the Mohawk at Fort Stanwix. After this I was a sergeant in the Cambridge militia, but we had no regular company enrolled, no regular officers. Men turned out when they pleased, and served under whom they pleased for the time [*they*] chose.

Fort Ann was simply a picket fort without ditch or earthy embankment around it. It was square and enclosed about half an acre's space. Within the fort was a single barrack, one story high, some sixteen feet wide and thirty or forty feet long—a framed and clapboarded building. Captain Adiel Sherwood of the Kingsbury militia with Lieutenant Thomas Bradshaw of the same place had command of this fort during the summer of Seventeen Hundred and Eighty. It was garrisoned by drafts and volunteers from the surrounding towns serving a month by turns. In September, I was there a month as sergeant with twelve privates from Cambridge under me. I would not consent to be drafted, but went up as a volunteer with the twelve men. The month expired and we returned, another file of men from Cambridge coming up to supply our places. The number of the garrison was variable, between fifty and one hundred men were always there.

[*In October 1780*] the alarm was sent and all the militia were ordered out to repel this invasion. We promptly rallied at Fort Edward, Colonel Yates being the commander of the militia there. Some two hundred of us went up to Fort George, and one of the officers of Warner's regiment—named Knowlton, if I remember right—went up from Fort Edward with us. We knew the enemy had fled and went up to bury the dead and secure any property that might be left. We found twenty-two slaughtered and mangled men. All had their skulls knocked in, their throats cut and their scalps taken. Their clothes were mostly stripped off.

101

The officer who came with us recognized Lieutenants Ensign and Eno and cried like a child at beholding them. They laid upon their backs, scalped and with their throats cut. Their stocks had been torn from their necks, the silver buckles taken from them, and the stocks were then laid across their breasts. We buried them both in one grave and buried all the men in graves not very deep in the sand.

One man only had not his throat coat; he was a mulatto and was lying on his face—the only one found in this posture. We supposed he was the drummer; and his arms were tied behind him with the cord of his drum, and he had been killed by a spear in his back after he was tied. There were six or eight spear wounds in the middle of his back, on each side of the back bone, and the spear was left in his back. He was scalped. We supposed he had been more obstinate and valiant in withstanding the enemy, and they had therefore bound and tortured him alive, as above intimated.

RUINS OF THE CITADEL OF FORT GEORGE.

The fort was still burning. A platform was erected in the fort on which a six-pounder mounted on a carriage was standing. One side of the platform was burnt away, and one of the wheels was so far burnt that the cannon had tipped partly down when we arrived. On the platform, not over three feet from the fire, was also standing a barrel filled with ball cartridges for muskets. These were quickly and eagerly divided among us.

All the enemy's killed were carried away. In a hollow, we observed the ground had just been filled in. On opening it, we found a British officer buried there with his clothes on. The Negro, above-mentioned, had his clothes all on; all the other bodies were stripped more or less. We buried them all a few rods to the west of where the road then ran. The fighting had been mostly with clubbed muskets, and the fragments of these, split and shivered, were laying around with the bodies. The barrel of one I observed had been bent full six inches from a straight line. This fort was never again repaired or garrisoned.[78]

One detail of Wells' account is corroborated by a letter of Major Carleton, himself. On November 6, 1780, Carleton wrote to the American Colonel Gansevoort about the battle at Fort George: "I heard of one man being killed after he was taken during the firing owing to a dispute between the two Indians of different villages who had taken him. He was either a Negro or a Stockbridge Indian, I believe, and he would not suffer himself to be conducted to the British guard by a Loyalist officer." *This must have been the black drummer found with bound hands and many spear wounds. Wells was surely right— that he had been tortured. Carleton's explanation of the incident does not deny this.*
Asa Fitch copied this letter from the original among Gansevoort's papers.[79]

To the End of the War

Though Mary Gillespie Bain does not date these memories, it is likely they come from the final years of the war.

Mary Gillespie Bain:

I have no scruples in telling what I know will help you in judging of the state of things here in the Revolutionary War. My father was a loyalist, as were all the other Argyle settlers. Father used to carry the packet or letters of intelligence from the Canadian officers to the British officers in New York. His part of the route was from here to Albany, commonly. A packet would be brought to him from the north, and he would forthwith start on with it to Albany. These

packets were done up in a small compass and enveloped in lead—being not more than an inch or two in length. He commonly received with them money enough only to pay his expenses. At the close of the war, the money was drawed by Patt Smyth to reward him liberally for his services, as had been promised, but Smyth cleared out and never paid him, preferring to keep the money himself.

I remember on one occasion, it was thought twould be difficult to get the packet through. Mother—who was Dutch, Father married at Wallkill—at this time put it into the middle of a biscuit, baking it carefully so as not to burn the paper in the middle. With this and a quantity of similar biscuits for his provisions on the journey, he started off. On his route, he fell in with a scouting party of American soldiers who were without provisions and hungry. They forthwith appropriated Father's biscuits to their own use. Father, now as they were eating the biscuit, regarded himself as a dead man. But to his joy, they returned it to him unbroken with a part of one or two other of the biscuits, having eaten all the rest. Why they passed this and broke all the others, I know not. Mother, in baking it, had been very careful not to heat it enough to burn the paper, and probably they observed it was poorly baked and heavy and therefore preferred all the others to this.

In the spring of the year, when making maple sugar, I and my older sister were one day in the woods keeping up the fire under the kettles, when I heard a whistle—the signal for calling Father. Speaking to my sister to listen, we soon heard it again clear and distinct. We forthwith sent to the house to let it be known. Lo, there was a scouting party of the Americans there, and young as we were, we knew it would not do to say anything in their hearing. So, crawling onto [Father's] lap I contrived to whisper in his ear "We have heard the whistle." On hearing what I said, he spoke, "Mother, get something for these children to eat. Mary says she is hungry; they have been left at the sugar camp so long. I will go and tend the kettles till they can go back to them." Father accordingly departed, having thus disarmed his guests.

There was much robbing of stock the last years of the Revolutionary War. The Whigs enlisted men for three months and six months to guard the frontier, and to pay these men, they would take cattle and sheep from the Argyle folks. I know that both cattle and sheep were taken from my father, two or three head at least at different times. The Salem Whigs made themselves rich in this way out of their Argyle neighbors—no restitution being made. But cattle and sheep that were taken down to Saratoga and Stillwater for supplying the army were all paid for afterwards.

The Tories also stole from their Whig neighbors when they were able to do so. Alexander Wright of Salem pilfered sheep from his neighbors' flocks till he collected a large flock. These he drove past my father's house and on to Burgoyne's camp where he sold them and got his pay in silver. But after the surrender, Captain Barnes of Salem commenced a suit against him in court. I remember Wright was over to Father's two or three times to see if he would not be willing to swear to such and such facts—but Father would not swear to all Wright wanted him to.[80]

Philip Lovelace was the true name of the "Lovett" mentioned below. His execution was one of the notable events of the Revolution in Schuylerville. Benjamin J. Lossings' Pictorial Fieldbook of the American Revolution *(New York, 1855) provides an account of Lovelace (not as interesting as Bitely's) as well as a view of his place of execution.*

Jacob Bitely:

That year [1781], I attended the execution of Lovett, the spy, at Schuylerville. He had previously resided about there and was well known to several. Lovett had gone in among the garrison at Schuylerville to spy it out and learn what the plans of the Whigs were. He was taken prisoner. Papers were found on him that showed he was commissioned to enlist men among the Tories in this quarter, to form a company and go to Canada. The papers certified that each man would receive a specified sum in silver on his arrival in Canada, in addition to what was paid down.

I guess it was in September when he was hung. It was the windiest day I ever saw. Of course, a large concourse of people was assembled. He was taken out of the guardhouse; his coffin was placed cross-wise on top of the box of a cart drawn by oxen, a rope around his neck, and a mulatto—slave of General Schuyler's, I think—holding the end of the rope, who made him walk close up to the cart. The guards surrounded him, forming a hollow square; thus they marched towards, half a mile, the gallows. The gallows was formed of two long, forked stakes drove into the ground and a pole placed across on the forks. The cart drove under the gallows and stopped. Lovett then got up into the cart, and also the minister who had attended with him after he was tried and sentenced. The minister, I think, was Mister Tanner, a Baptist, who was preaching then up Battenkill. He talked and prayed with him, then shook hands with him and bade him farewell—both standing up in the cart—and then descended.

The Negro then tied the rope to the pole; the cart drove out from under him and he hung till he was dead. Then he was cut down [and] the guards now marched away. The Negro took off the white frock which he had on over his clothes. He then twitched his silver shirt sleeve buttons and pocketed them; next stripped off his vest; then took hold of the bottoms of his pantaloons and with a violent yank, which drew the body a foot or two forwards, pulled them off and exposed his legs. Some of the spectators could endure the Negro's brutality no longer. They kicked him and forbade his taking off the shirt from the corpse. So the Negro desisted.[81]

Mary Gillespie Bain:

Lovett was at our house, and stayed in our barn overnight the third day before he was hung on a tree at Schuylerville. Two other men were in company with him at the same time. He was as fine a looking man as I ever saw.[82]

According to histories of New York State, the last battle of the Revolution fought in the state was at Johnstown in October of 1781. The following account shows the dangers of life in this frontier county even very late in the war.

Jacob Bitely:

In the spring of Seventeen Hundred and Eighty-two, a party of Tory refugees who had sold out and left this part of the country was dispatched from Canada to come down and capture some of the Whigs in this neighborhood [*Fort Edward*]. The party was about twenty in number. Thomas Sherwood was their captain, William Saunders and George Campbell was among them. Saunders afterwards told me their orders from the Canadian officers were not to molest any quiet or neutral inhabitants but to seize and carry off those who were most active in the Whig interest and who had been the most troublesome to the loyalists in this neighborhood.

The party came up the lake in two boats, and hiding them, came secretly over to their friends here. They stayed out in Argyle and none here knew of their being down. Francis De Long was the main agent in furthering their designs. They did not want to take the men from their houses amid the shrieks and tears of the females and children. So De Long—who lived on the road to Argyle where the Fort Edward and Durkeetown Roads come together—in order to get the men separate from their families, came out here to buy fish. It was then the season for shad fishing. He said he wanted the men to go out that night and catch all the fish they could, and he would come down the next morning and pay for them—he and his neighbors wanting them.

Thus deceived, my two brothers John and Henry Bitely, Silas Bristol, Thomas Durkee, and Ezra Swain went out together to draw the seine on Rogers Bar, as it is since called, a mile and a half above here. It was a bright, moonlit night, the Eighteenth of June, Seventeen Hundred and Eighty-two. As they threw out their net and were pulling in towards shore in the boat to land and draw the net in, the party, who had by this time secreted themselves upon the shore, suddenly rose up, presented their guns and ordered them to come ashore and surrender or everyone of them was a dead man. Not far off was a vacant house in which Bristol had lived, and adjoining this house he had this season, commenced raising a field of corn. They took the prisoners to this house. Bristol had left the harness with which he had done his plowing. They cut up the harness, and with it securely tied the five captives, and set three or four of their number to guard them.

The remainder of the party now started down the river for Ephraim Crocker's. He and his family were all in bed when the party reached his house. They took him, his brother Levi Crocker, Elijah Dunham, and also a Continental soldier that happened to be there and who was in bed in one of the chambers at the time. They now marched off with their prisoners for Canada, nine in number.

Elijah Dunham was a young man and he begged of them with tears and sobs to let him go. He said he was to be married to Miss Cassel of Kingsbury. The day was set and near at hand for their wedding; but this he did not regard so much as the fact that if he was carried off, the girl would be disgraced. They had been guilty of a misstep; marriage only could save her with reputation. On reaching the lake where their boats lay, having exacted from him the most full and solemn promises never to fight against the King or in any way molest those who were friends to the royal cause, they released him.

The other captives were put in the boats and proceeded down the lake. At Dutchman's Point, which is on the west shore of Lake Champlain, they landed and left the boats; they were within the British lines, as Saint Leger with his force was then encamped on an island in the lake opposite this point.

109

From here they marched barefoot from Chambly to Montreal. Durkee was loaded with two packs upon his back and his feet soon became so sore and cut upon the stones that he could be tracked at every step by the blood that ran from them.

They were finally taken to Cote du Lac Island. A large number of American prisoners were there confined and underwent the greatest privations. Not even straw was furnished them to sleep on. I well remember my brother's saying when he got home that his old hat had been his only pillow; his clothes, his sole bed and bedding, all the time he was in prison. They were all alive, moreover, with vermin. And their diet the chief part of the time was sea-biscuit and spoiled beef. The biscuit was old and hard enough to almost strike fire like a flint. They could only use it by boiling it a long time with a slice of the beef and thus making it into a kind of soup. So hard was their fare, they looked more like ghosts or skeletons than men. Old Eben Fuller was captured in Kingsbury and carried to Cote du Lac Island. At the surrender of Fort Ann, his son Nathan was taken and sent to the same island; but his father was so changed that the son wholly failed of recognizing him, and could scarcely be persuaded that the person before him was his father.

At length peace was restored, and the prisoners were taken out, as winter was approaching, to be sent home. Some of them were fearful that stress of weather or some other thing would be pled as an excuse for taking them to England, when once on shipboard, and staying with them there till the next season opened. Full of these apprehensions, the two Crockers and Thomas Durkee ran away. The guard soon discovered their absence and pursued after them; but they found a boat and pushed across the river in it, and the guard gave over the pursuit. They came up the west side of the Sorel nearly to Lake Champlain, and there crossed the river in an old battoe and came down through Vermont. All the settlements in Vermont were broken up, and without shoes and but half clothed, they suffered everything—subsisting upon frogs, birches, sorrel, wintergreens, et cetera, wading through swamps and sleeping in the open air in the frosts of December. Crocker's

110

feet were ever after tormenting him with chilblains caused by this journey, but they finally got home alive.

The vessel on which my brothers embarked was loaded with prisoners. The first days out, the vessel was almost logged with ice by night. Then came on a violent storm, which nearly wrecked them, and drove them into so warm a climate that they were fainting with the heat. At length they reached New York. Here the vessel stopped and discharged all the prisoners that belonged south. An officer, with whom one of my brothers had got well acquainted, was very earnest to have him leave the vessel and go home and live with him in ease and comfort in Carolina, but Brother preferred coming home. The vessel then came up the river, but could only get to Dobbs Ferry, on account of the ice. Here the northern prisoners were landed. From the soldiers in the Highlands, they got some old coarse shoes, and came on homewards on foot, so covered with lice they could not ask of the inhabitants a bed to sleep in. They slept in barns or on the floors of houses, but the folks on the way supplied them with enough to eat. They reached home upon the last day of December, the same year they were taken, and the next day was a happy New Year to us, as you may readily suppose.[83]

PART THREE:

A NEW COUNTY

AFTERMATH OF WAR

John Pattison was an uncle of Asa Fitch. He was born in 1778 in Stillwater.

John Pattison:

Noah Payne [*of Fort Miller*] was never taken prisoner, but Ephraim Crocker was. Mister Wing, grandfather to the present Daniel Wing of Fort Edward, was the ringleader in capturing him and took him to Montreal and delivered him up to the jailer there. But Crocker broke jail before long and returned, freezing his feet or two of his toes when on his way home.

When Wing delivered Crocker to the Montreal jailer and left him, Crocker said something to this effect to Wing: "My curse upon you, Wing! I shall yet live to see you in as secure a place as this." After a long series of years had passed away, Wing committed forgery, was convicted and sent to the state's prison at New York. Now was Crocker's hour of triumph. He rode up to my store one morning for some tobacco, et cetera, which he needed to complete his outfit, put them in his saddle bags, flung them over his saddle, mounted and started away for New York on a brisk trot—the saddle bags going slap-slap-slap against the horse's sides and Crocker's arms flapping up and down with the horse's motion as though he was actually flying. He rode all the way to New York on purpose to see Wing there and remind him of their parting at Montreal jail.[84]

Daniel Carswell:

I was born in Colerain [*Massachuetts*] and was four years old when Father moved to Salem in the year Seventeen Hundred and Seventy-nine. My brother Abner enlisted for nine months and was stationed at Fort Ann. [*My brother*]

115

David went up to Fort Ann to take Abner's place and let him come home for a short time. Whilst David was there as Abner's substitute, Fort Ann was taken [*by Carleton*], and David was carried prisoner to Canada. Caldwell of Cambridge, Cowan and many others were taken. They were at first confined in Montreal jail. My brother and five others broke jail at one time and made their escape, getting down to Co--os in Vermont. They deemed all danger of recapture past and struck up a fire where they encamped at night. This led to their being discovered by a scouting party, by whom they were taken back to Canada. They were now handcuffed and sent to an island in the Saint Lawrence rapids nine miles above Montreal [*Cote du Lac*]. Here they were guarded by American Tories who were tenfold more unkind to them than Indians would have been. Although the river was running but a few rods from the prison, they at one time would not give them any water, till some of the men became so dry and thirsty they were attacked with raising of the blood. At length, my brother was exchanged and came home.

A few years after the peace, one Yarnes, a Tory—I think he had been living in Kingsbury—came to Salem when court was sitting, to get compensation for some land that had been unjustly confiscated. My brother was in the courtroom one day and, seeing Yarnes, went to him and asked him if he knew him. Yarnes pretended he did not. "Don't you remember when I was a prisoner in Canada and perishing of thirst, you was one of the guards?" My brother knew he could not be mistaken in the man, and having a whip in his hand, struck him to the floor with the butt of it. A constable was ordered to protect Yarnes out of the court, but he had no sooner got into the hall than he received another blow. Getting into the street he was beset by a crowd who kicked, cuffed, and pounded him without mercy until he was entirely out of the village.[85]

Donald McDonald:

James Rogers was a noted deer hunter and had a long gun with which he made sure shot at a great distance. He sent word to Simpson's family, when John was reported to be with them on a visit, that he [*Simpson*] must keep out of reach of his long gun.[86]

In October, 1848, Dr. Fitch interviewed Mr. Weller, "a surveyor living one mile northeast of Fort Ann Village." For Weller's generation, born after the Revolution, relics and memories of the war were only curiosities.

Mr. Weller:

Seven or eight of the British killed in the encounter of July Eighth, Seventeen Hundred and Seventy-seven [*when Burgoyne took Fort Ann*] were buried near the summit of Battle Hill. Major Beach, who was in the engagement, settled in Benson, Vermont. He used to come down here almost every year, for several years in succession when he was an old man, and spend a day or two with Father, who owned the land, in walking over its ground and relating what he recollected of the battle. Major Beach pointed out the burial spot on the hill. On digging down where he said, we found six or eight skulls, bones enough to fill a bushel basket, leather stocks, et cetera. These we reinterred on the same spot except one skull; this had a bullet hole in it a little above the right eye. The bullet entered the frontal sinus and pursued it upwards, separating the two tables of the skull a few inches and was still remaining wedged in the skull in that situation, flattened nearly as thin as a half-dollar piece. I took this skull to New York, in Eighteen Hundred and Seventeen, and deposited it in Peale's Museum, receiving a free admission ticket to the museum therefore while I stayed in New York.[87]

TROUBLES AND EMBARRASSMENTS

The years following the Revolution were not easy ones for many people. Almost everyone who spoke to Dr. Fitch about these times mentions money or land troubles of some kind: problems with taxes, bankruptcies, disputed land titles, etc. The questions about many deeds came from the casual arrangements of some first settlers. Bankruptcies affected both "big" people and "little" people.

Robert Hanna (b. 1770) was living in Salem in 1786—the year of Shays' uprising. Shays' Rebellion had sympathizers in this county, and though Robert Hanna doesn't tell us this, Shays and some followers actually hid out for several years in Sandgate, Vermont—directly across the Washington County border. Reportedly, Shays was helped by two Salem men, James McCracken and Nathan Wilson, to set up an outlaw village there on top of Egg Mountain.[88]

Robert Hanna:

I was too young to be called into service in the Revolution, but when I was sixteen years old I was ordered out to quell the rebellion in Granville. Isaac Mitchell was the sergeant of the company who warned me. The captain was old James Stewart or else Armstrong—I ain't certain which. I did not go, but quite a party from Salem did go. The rebellion did not amount to much. It was some men there who would not pay taxes. It was in Shays' time, I remember. Who any of their names were I do not know. But they gave up when they heard the militia were on their way up so it was all settled and over with before the militia got there.

Shays, when he was driven out of Massachusetts, fled through this town. He came here on a stud horse which was so fatigued and jaded out that he was anxious to exchange it for a fresh one, and Sam McCarter traded with him and continued to own this stud horse that he got of Shays a number of years.[89]

John McEachron was born in 1771 "in the Highlands down the Hudson River—somewhere between Albany and New York." His mother was a Dutch woman, Katy Acker. John thought that his father, Neal McEachron, one of Laughlin Campbell's colony, was probably born in the New York Highlands, too.

John McEachron:

My Father came here [*Argyle*] with his family in Seventeen Hundred and Seventy-five, settling on the next lot north of where I live—Lot Number Thirty-seven. He did not draw the land but bought it of one Von Bleck, I think his name was. This lot contained three hundred acres. He put up a house where my nephew William Livingston now lives. Father's brother, Peter McEachron, came here several years before Father did. I think he did not draw a lot in town but bought of someone. He put up a house of round logs first, and afterward a larger, better one of squared logs which is still standing at the head of the lake. Peter's son Daniel has several times threatened to drive me off from this lot, claiming it as his and his brothers' from their father. None of us have any original claim to it and I hold it only by possession. My uncle McNight was one of the surveyors in running out the town, and he told Father that if he would take possession of this lot no one would ever appear to molest him, it being but a fragmentary corner of a hundred acres, the rest of it being covered by the lake. So I put up a house and have always lived here.[90]

119

William McCollister:

When the town came to be divided into lots, and the lots were drawn by the proprietors, the lot on which my father [*Hamilton McCollister*] had cleared and put up his house was drawn by McCrelis. Father made a bargain with McCrelis for the lot—was to give him forty dollars for it, I suppose, for this was the common price at which the proprietors held their lots. Ere Father paid and took a deed of the lot, McCrelis died and Father paid his widow and took a deed from her or some other title.

About the breaking out of the Revolutionary War, he sold the lot, Number One Hundred and Seventy, to old Doctor John Williams for two hundred and fifty dollars. Sometime after, McCrelis' heirs, three boys, came of age and immediately came up and threatened ejecting Williams if he did not buy of them. If old Mister Pennel who lived on John McDonald's place had not set them on, it would have been easily got along with, for their claim would be outlawed in three or four weeks—which fact Pennel made known to them, so there was no putting them off. Father never forgot this unneighborly act in neighbor Pennel. The McCrelis heirs demanded five hundred dollars. Williams paid half this sum, Father the other half—thus losing forty dollars in cash besides his improvements on Lot Number One Hundred and Seventy.[91]

Catherine Boyd was the widow of Robert Boyd; he was born in 1756 in Ireland and came to Salem with his parents in 1773. Boyd was a member of Barnes' scout during the Revolution.

Catherine Boyd:

My husband became involved [*sic*] in consequence of drink and dissipation and sold out here and bought a miserable farm on Canada line in the town of Champlain. We lived there seven years and came from there in time of the late war—after Plattsburgh battle. The land was so poor we could not even raise provision enough for our own eating off from it. We fairly starved out on it. My own brother was captain of a company of engineers in the Canadian Army, receiving sixty dollars per month. He urged us to move into Canada and he would give us a good farm and make us comfortable, but my husband would not venture to go there—fearing some rebellious word against royalty and the King might escape us and lead us into danger.[92]

THE STORY OF BETSEY MUNRO

The downfall of Betsey Munro, the beloved daughter of Harry Munro, was one result of the dislocations following the war, though Betsey's own character obviously had a lot to do with her troubles.

Donald McDonald:

The Jay family lived in Rye and it was there that he [*Harry Munro*] married his second wife, who was a sister of Governor Jay. He had removed from here when he married her. By her he had one son, Peter Jay Munro. He had none of that affection for his second wife that he had had for his first. He adored his first wife and after her death transferred his affections to the daughter [*Betsey*] letting her go unrestrained and thus spoiling her.[93]

George Webster:

Munro had two children by two wives viz. Peter Jay Munro and Betsey. Betsey was a perfectly reckless devil—full of all sorts of mischief and deviltry, breaking dishes in the house and destroying everything she could lay her hands on when the whim took her. On one occasion she scared John Duncan's wife almost to death. She was in some low bushes in the neighborhood, and seeing Duncan's wife coming she threw her clothes up all over her head, and on all fours advanced backwards, bum foremost, in the path towards Mistress Duncan.

She was always rambling about the country and spent much time at William Reid's and Peter McQueen's of Fitch's Point. She was there when she was married. Donald Fisher was her husband. He was an awkward boorish fellow in his manners but otherwise a worthy person. He was a tailor by trade and owned a farm over east of Munro's on Indian River and was in very good circumstances. I think likely Doctor Clark married them.[94]

Donald McDonald:

Donald Fisher was at first a tailor in the city of New York. He there bought of one Kennith McKinnith the lands originally granted to Byrne [*in Granville*]. Fisher got several of his relatives over from Scotland and they all came up and settled on his lands.

Donald Fisher married Betsey Munro as stated by George Webster. Her father was very averse to this match and felt cold towards Esquire Reid ever afterwards for allowing the marriage to be at his house and favored by him.

When the Revolutionary War was in progress, Munro got permission of the authorities to go to Canada. From thence he never returned but went over to England and Scotland and died at Edinburgh in Eighteen Hundred and One or Two. We always supposed that he received pay from the English government for his lands here, for he must have had money from this source to support him after he left this country. He moreover only gave to his son Peter Jay Munro a quitclaim of the patent. Peter Jay sold out his rights to the soil immediately after his father's death, about the years Eighteen Hundred and One or Two. I was his agent in most of this business.

Fisher also went off to Canada in the war, and his lands here were confiscated and sold. Mistress Betsey Fisher did not accompany her husband to Canada. Indeed she only lived with him as the fit took her. After he went away she resided in a house of her own at the Meadows on Lot Eighteen.

She contested her half-brother Peter Jay Munro's title to her father's lands, founding her claim upon a pretended deed given to her by her father shortly before he went from Canada to England. Peter Jay Munro had her arrested for forgery. She was taken from her house here at the Meadows in November, Eighteen Hundred, and carried down to Albany jail.

It was the tenth day of March, Eighteen Hundred and One, that I started from here with a load of witnesses to attend the court in Albany for Peter Jay Munro. She was tried by Judge Lansing, and the evidence of her guilt was conclusive. It was proved that her deed was dated after her father left Canada. The two witnesses to the deed were both subpoenaed down from Canada and both swore that their names had been forged. But most conclusive of all was the water lines in the paper on which the deed was written. The date of the deed was some years previous to the date when the paper was manufactured.

The proof was so strong that she was brought in guilty and was sentenced to the state prison for life. But after lying in prison awhile, she was pardoned out and her brother hired a Mister Hubbs to take her to Canada. She there married a second husband and lived at Missisco Bay, but after a while she parted from her husband. She then taught a school in Montreal, and at length, died in that city.

She had two sons and one daughter [by Fisher]. Elizabeth, the daughter, I took to Canada in Eighteen Hundred and Two by direction of Peter Jay Munro, and left her with a Mistress Thompson in Montreal. She was then eighteen years old; was fair looking but not such a keen, black-eyed person as her mother.[95]

The statements of George Webster and Donald McDonald give a sparse outline of an unusual life. Betsey Munro Fisher tells more—definitely not all—in a small, rare book entitled The Memoirs of Mrs. Elizabeth Fisher, *privately printed in New York City between 1807 and 1809. (A sole copy survives in the Huguenot–Thomas Paine Society Library in New Rochelle). This 48-page history is an amazing account of dramatic meetings and battles with her father, husband, and brother, lawsuits, desperate sleigh rides with sheriffs at her heels, shipwrecks (Lake Champlain), prison—plus many hints of sexual scandal. Amidst this saga of a true-life Moll Flanders, Betsey sets us straight on some facts: 1) John Jay's sister was Munro's third wife. Betsey briefly had another stepmother who died. 2) If a Mr. Hobbs did take Betsey to Canada when she was released from prison, she immediately returned and lived for some time in New York City and also at the Meadows—before going back to Canada.*

FALL OF THE HOUSE OF DUER

William Duer was the founder of the village of Fort Miller— so called from the military buildings on the west shore of the river put up during the French and Indian War. He was a British ex-officer with aristocratic connections and a very important person in the county before and during the Revolution. He served as one of the first judges of the county (when it was still called Charlotte County) and held court at his fine house in Fort Miller. Unlike another rich and powerful patentee, Philip Skene, Duer took the American side in the war and was active in New York State revolutionary councils.

John Pattison:

I first went from home in Seventeen Hundred and Ninety-six to serve as a clerk to Hugh Pebbles whose store was three miles north of Waterford. In Seventeen Hundred and Ninety-eight I came here to Fort Miller with Gerrit Pebbles, brother to Hugh, as his clerk and stayed one year.

William Duer, Senior, I think, was born in England and married a daughter of Lord Stirling's. After the war his family lived here, I know. He speculated largely after the war in government securities—so largely that some thought that he meant to own the government—but he was unable to meet his liabilities and thus became a ruined man. When he failed his estate was inventoried and amounted to a hundred and thirty thousand pounds. He was committed to prison in New York and laid there some years. Finally he got released from jail, took cold and died ten days after his enlargement.

The Duer mansion had such an air of baronial splendor, I used to delight to go over the river and sit down and look at it. It was so far back from the top of the hill that it could be but partially seen on this side of the river. The main building was fifty-two feet square, two stories high, and a high basement. The roof was four-square and was flattish and surrounded with a balustrade, with a scuttle door to go out onto it. On the east front was a piazza, two stories high, the upper piazza having a bedroom enclosed off from each end; the lower piazza was open its entire length of fifty-two feet. On each side was a wing twenty-two feet square. The wings stood fourteen feet from the main building, the intervening space being also enclosed. The windows were large and the whole was finished off in a style of elegance such as I had never seen before, I having at that date been no farther south than Albany.

I am surprised that it was pulled down. No one at this day would demolish such a building. But the timber of some of it was wanted for a building or two down here at the falls. And having been unoccupied for a year or two or more, some worthless scamps of the neighborhood had made free to injure it. The window casings were torn off and the leaden weights by which the windows were hung were stolen from every one of the windows. The sheet lead in the gutters of the roofs was also all cut away; in short, whatever any of these

125

fellows had found that they wanted, they had made free to take. The edifice thus becoming so marred and dilapidated, it was taken down by Pebbles.

I measured it all by his directions and was for some time occupied in drawing out and straightening the wrought nails from the boards. This work at first I did not fancy at all. But getting used to it, it became a pleasure to me. The iron was so tough, they would be drawn out and straightened so prettily that it was a pastime to me, and I regretted it when it was completed that I had no more such work to do.[96]

THE ANGELS: A FAMILY OUTLINE

Some things about Tryphena Angel's life seem very modern: frequent moves and the scattering of her grandchildren across two states—New York and Wisconsin.

Tryphena Martin Angel:

When sixteen years old, I married Augustus Angel. He was born at Chockset in Massachusetts. After the war he came up to Hoosic—was a carpenter and millright by trade, was employed much in putting up mills. He built Carter's sawmill below McNab's Lake on the Cossayuna Creek, and a year or two after, was employed by Conkey to build him a fulling mill here on Fitch's Point. It was here that I got acquainted with him and married him. He then made arrangements with Father [*Moses Martin*] to build a dam and sawmill at East Greenwich, when Father suddenly died and Walter Martin then went into partnership with him in the enterprise. He put up the dam, the first dam that was built at East Greenwich, and the sawmill on the Jackson side of the stream, and also built the bridge above the dam which ever went by the name of Angel's Bridge till it fell and drowned a child of William Taylor's.

He got the land on the Jackson side of the kill from Banyar in New York. We lived there eight or ten years when he became so embarrassed that we had to give it up. We moved to West Haven in Vermont, a mile or two north of the tavern

126

and church, where we lived twenty-five years. We then moved to Chester in Warren County where we lived twenty-four years. We next came to Ticonderoga to live with our granddaughter; Mister Angel sickened and died within a fortnight after our arrival there.

Our only child was Newell Angel. He had two wives, both of West Haven, and six children now living by each wife. He is now living in Milwaukee, Wisconsin—if alive. His children are as follows: Augustus, living at Malone, Michigan—has three or four children; William Harrison, married Lavinia Abernethy of New Haven, Vermont and lives at Sun Prairie, Wisconsin—two children; Sarah Eliza, married Franklin Prouty and lives at Galesville, New York and has one child; Chester Fitch, unmarried, worked last summer at the MacIntyre iron works in Essex County; Lydia Almira, married Austin Skinner and lives at Ticonderoga—I live with her—she has two children, girls; George Newell, married Palmira Warren who died leaving one child—he lives at Ticonderoga Falls; Harriet, died at Chester, Warren County; Ransom died at Chester; Charles, in Wisconsin with his father; Rowland Mallory, lives in Chester; Caroline, in Chester, wife of Lyman Duel; Franklin, in Wisconsin with his father; Frederick, in Wisconsin with his father; Ransom ditto.[97]

WORK OF THE COUNTY

Samuel Cook:

I was born at Stillwater in Seventeen Hundred and Seventy-nine. My father Jacob Cook moved from there to this place [*Fort Edward*] in Seventeen Hundred and Eighty-eight. When we came here there were but four houses standing in Fort Edward: two framed and two log houses.

The fort was then quite perfect, though dilapidated. Three blockhouses were built as outposts on the surrounding hills. One was on the other side of the river, west of the dam. Another was southeast from the fort on the hill in front of Colonel Fort's house. The third was on the hill, north of the village, beside the road to Forts Ann and George. This was standing quite perfect when I came here. It was built of squared timber, the corners dovetailed together and roofed with boards and perforated with portholes large enough to run out the muzzle of a cannon. It was a large structure, the outline of which is still visible by a slight depression in the ground.

When Father came here, our grinding was done at Gillis' Mill five miles from here on Mud Creek, a branch of Wood Creek, in the northwest corner of Argyle. But most of the Indian corn for our johnnycakes was ground by hand, in a mortar at the Bell place north of the village. A stump here had been burnt hollow by red hot cannon balls dropped onto it thus forming a mortar; and the pestle was a long round stone hung to a limb of a tree which bent down with the weight of the stone pestle allowing it to play in the mortar.

I well remember the next year after we came here, Moses Harris of Queensbury killed a panther thus. He had two fine hogs fatted. One morning one of them was missing from the pens. It had been carried off by a panther who had partly devoured it and concealed the remainder by covering it with some leaves in the woods. Harris searched and found the carcase. He hereupon fixed his gun with a cord, tied to the carcase and reaching to the trigger of the gun, and left it thus. The following night the panther returned to feast upon the hog; and so skillfully had Harris arranged his apparatus that the gun went off and killed the panther. Harris brought the panther down here to Fort Edward where it was exhibited to all the inhabitants—this being at that date the most considerable place in this vicinity.

Originally wolves thronged the Kingsbury swamp, and this remained their haunt for years after they had been exterminated in all the surrounding country. They were such an annoyance that in Eighteen Hundred and One a great wolf hunt was had, all the inhabitants gathering on a specified day and surrounding the swamp. The number killed on this occasion was either nine or eleven, I am not certain which. This broke them up so that after, there was no further trouble from them, though two or three remained in the swamp a few years longer. The leader of the wolf hunt was Thomas Sherwood's father, Adiel.[98]

John McEachron:

I know nothing of any panthers having been killed about here. Wolves used to be plenty and sometimes the sheep, when chased by them, would run directly into the house if the door was left open.

Rattlesnakes still [1847] abound on the hills between here and Bedlam, and one, two, or four are killed every year. Bears used to be in the woods also. I remember on one occasion when our cattle came home from the woods at night, a two-year old steer was missing. Father went out to search for it and, near where Andrus Weaver's house now stands, found it and a large bear that had killed and was eating it. He got word to the Gillis boys near the Corners and they came over with their dogs and guns. As they approached the bear, he sat himself up on his haunches with his back against a large tree, and the dogs went at him. But with his paws he would knock them hither and thither as fast as they came within his reach. The men had some difficulty in firing at him, the dogs beset him so on every side. They fired as they had chances for doing it without hurting the dogs; and it was not until they had put thirteen bullets through his hide that he was killed. He weighed twelve or thirteen hundred pounds. His head, elevated on the top of a pole, was exhibited a number of years beside the road at my Uncle Peter's.[99]

Donald McDonald:

I was about nineteen years old [1787] when we took our first load of wheat to Lansingburgh. The road went about where the present road goes from Munro's Meadows past West Hebron and down the creek past Fitch's Point. It went over Campbell's Hill in Greenwich, which was by far the heaviest hill upon the route, thence down to Galesville where we crossed Battenkill. Then out to DeRidders where we went onto the ice of the river and continued on it down to Bemis Heights, thence through Stillwater, the Borough—Mechanicville—and Half-Moon.

It required three days to take a load to market and return home. Twenty bushels of wheat were always taken as a load. I was about the first one, I suppose, that showed the folks that more could be taken. Having a good and true team, I was sure I could take more with ease and so put on twenty-five bushels. Going up the Campbell Hill, I told the man ahead of me that I had on twenty-five bushels. It was thought so remarkable a load that he halloed to the man forward of him, telling him the fact. And thus the announcement was passed forward from one team to another on the long train upon the road that "There was a fellow behind who had got on twenty-five bushels!"[100]

Donald McDonald:

Potatoes were brought here and cultivated when we first came. The early settlers, to economize as much as possible, always sliced the seed. The slices were dropped three or four inches apart around a foot or more and covered with the hoe forming a hill so large around as a bushel basket. No further cultivation was bestowed upon them till they were harvested.

The Spanish potato was the kind first here. It was watery and of an inferior quality but yielded well. Some ten years after, the yellow Rusty-Coats were introduced. These were a round potato with a rough skin and generally cracking open when boiled. Then the Rusty-Coat-Reds. These were small, few of them being larger than a hen's egg—fine for roasting and as white and mealy as flour inside but could not be used for boiling as they would crack all to pieces. These are all gone now. I have not seen one of them in thirty years. [McDonald made this statement in 1847.]

Next the Red potato came into the country. These were often six inches long and as large around as my wrist, of a deep red color, keeping well late in the spring and yielding well—sometimes producing three or four hundred bushels per acre. When I worked the farm of Peter Jay Munro at Mamaroneck in Westchester County I raised nearly this quanitiy, though from the smallest and most inferior quality of seed.

The Leopards were introduced here thirty or forty years ago. The Orange potato I brought into this country in Eighteen Hundred and Five from New Lebanon. The Shakers there were raising this kind largely at that time. The Long Johns were introduced about twenty years ago. They want rich land and early planting.[101]

SHEEP

There was a lot of interest in sheep-raising here in the first part of the nineteenth century. Unfortunately, after an early boom in wool prices during the War of 1812, prices went steadily down, as Alexander Livingston admits below at the end of this account of his career as a sheep farmer and breeder.

Alexander Livingston:

The first full-blooded Merino buck that was brought into Washington County was from Humphrey's flock in Connecticut. It was brought here by Nathan Wilson up White Creek. I believe Wilson got a premium of one hundred dollars that was given, I suppose, by the state for the first full-blood buck introduced into each of the counties.

Next after this was the McNish bucks, three in number, belonging to Robert Prince, a merchant of New York. The first two of these came to Salem in the fall or summer of Eighteen Hundred and Ten. They were imported sheep and McNish had certificates of each of them, but I remember only one—that was certified to be a Paular Merino. His throat was smooth, or at least had nothing of that enormous dewlap now belonging to the Paulars, and the wool was good on the hips. The second was probably a Paular also, had coarse hips but little of a dewlap. The third was some other variety. I know not what. It was the largest buck of the three, whitest, the wool long but very thin, the fleece weighing less than six pounds.

In the fall of Eighteen Hundred and Eleven, I hired Number One of McNish for one season for fifty dollars, and was restricted to put but fifty ewes to him of the common sheep of the country. From the fifty ewes I raised but twenty lambs. The fleeces of these half-bloods averaged three and one-third pounds each. In Eighteen Hundred and Sixteen, the sixth [year] I had been in business, I got the first full-blood Merino ewe I ever owned from [Isaac] Bishop of Granville.

My next ewes I got thus. Being in New York in Eighteen Hundred and Twenty, in a storehouse, I observed a quantity of fine wool. I selected some of the nicest and inquired where it was grown. They told me in Long Island by the Quakers. There were four within three miles of each other in Queens County that had the choicest-fleeced Merino sheep in the country: Judge Effingham Lawrence, Andrew Cook, Timothy Matlet, and Silas Titus. As I afterwards learned, Lawrence had bid off three of the choicest ewes in the New York market for the enormous sum of three thousand dollars—kept one himself, Matlet took one, and Cook the other. Cook's soon after died and he pointed me once to a spot in his yard where he said he had lost one thousand dollars—alluding to the death of this ewe. Having learned of these men, I went down in the fall of Eighteen Hundred and Twenty and got four full-blood ewes and buck lambs of Cook. They cost me five dollars per head.

In the fall of Eighteen Hundred and Twenty-two, I went down again and bought forty-eight ewe lambs of Cook for five dollars and fifty cents per head and two buck lambs from Lawrence. To get them home cost me about a dollar per head, four shillings being the price on the sloop from New York to Troy. The steamboat would not take them. Daniel Cleveland of Salem had about fifty lambs on the same sloop he had bought from Cook.

These were all the Merino ewes I ever bought and from them my present flock has been derived. I never owned but one Saxon ewe.

In Eighteen Hundred and Twenty-five, I went with Esquire David Campbell of Jackson to the great sale of Saxon bucks at Brighton, July Fourteenth. We made a close examination and took samples of some twenty one and two-year-old bucks—which samples I still have—on which we concluded we would bid and secure some one of them. But they went so extravagantly high that we bought none. Four hundred and fifty dollars was given for a one-year-old buck and everyone went for three hundred dollars—save one so old his teeth were already poor. I told Campbell we might congratulate ourselves on that day's sales; it would flood the country with Saxon bucks and we could soon get them cheap enough.

My present flock is something over two hundred. About seventy of these are nearly pure Saxon and about the same number are pure Merino. The rest are grades between.

I once weighed the fleeces of eleven Merino and also of twelve of my best Saxon ewes, lambs shorn for the first time. Each weighed precisely the same—thirty-five pounds. Were I without any sheep and about to purchase a flock, I do not know if I should have any preference between the Merino and Saxon. The Saxons are the cleanest, prettiest looking sheep, and it is pleasant keeping such a flock, but one is just about as profitable as the other as the market price for wool always ranges. Sheep of a lower quality than full blood Merino I should not think of purchasing.

During the War of Eighteen Hundred and Twelve to Fifteen, full-blood Merino wool was worth about two dollars per pound. Half-Merino I sold to Luther Binel, a manufacturer at Fitch's Point, Salem, for one dollar per pound. On the close of the war the prices fell some four or five shillings per pound. But there was no market for wool in the country at that day; it could not be turned into money except occasionally. Had it made into cloth and sold in stores, et cetera.

About Eighteen Hundred and Twenty and Twenty-one, I sent clips to New York City. My flock was then a high grade of Merino. I sold for five shillings per pound the first I took there. The finest Long Island wool was then bringing six shillings per pound—the Quaker lots from Queens County.

Eighteen Hundred and Twenty-five, I sold for fifty-two cents to Bishop and Stevens who bought extensively at that time. Stevens lived in Shaftsbury, Vermont.

Eighteen Hundred and Twenty-seven, sold to the same for thirty-six cents. This was the first of any regular market in our own county.

Eighteen Hundred and Thirty-one, sold two clips to Goodrich of Bellows Falls for one dollar. The preceding autumn Raymond, cashier of Manchester Bank, had offered me seventy-five cents which I refused. Many this year refused to sell and made a great mistake in thus refusing.

Eighteen Hundred and Thirty-two, sold to Barker of White Creek for fifty-two cents. My wool was now Saxon-Merino. Esquire Campbell, Constant Clapp and John Dobbin at this time sold for the same price—these being the choicest flocks at that date in the county. We wouldn't have sold for that price but the cholera had just broke out in the country and we were afraid it would stop the manufactories at the east and cut off the sale of wool.

Sold for forty cents for a few of the last years.[102]

Constant Clapp was the founder of Clapp's Mills, later called Rexleigh Mills in Salem.

Constant Clapp, Esquire:

Several of Humphrey's imported Merinos were sent to Stoddard [*of Rupert, Vermont*] to be kept on his farm soon after they arrived in this country. Grade bucks from Stoddard's flock were bought by Amherst Wheeler, Esquire of Salem, Judge McLean of Jackson and others. Some of this half-blood Merino wool I manufactured in the year of Eighteen Hundred and Six and made wretched work of it—all the carding machines in the country were quite too coarse for Merino wool.

Previous to the Merinos, the Otter sheep were brought into Boston by Lord Selkirk. They were deformed looking things, with wool about as fine as the better kinds of common sheep then in the country. As they could not jump—their legs turning out as if they had been broken—many thought they would be better than our common sheep. There has never been but an occasional specimen of this breed in the county.

The Revolutionary soldiers that were present at the siege of Yorktown used to talk much of the big-tailed sheep they there saw—their tails weighing fifteen and sometimes as high as seventeen pounds. And to keep them out of the dirt, little truck wheels were placed under them which the sheep drew about presenting a most comical sight to northern eyes. The statement I have so often heard, and from men who said they had seen it, that there is no doubt of its truth.[103]

Thomas Dickison was born in 1770 in Greenwich "on the banks of Battenkill about half a mile below Hardscrabble [Centre Falls]." His family had come to the town that same year from Rhode Island.

Thomas Dickison:

None of the Bald Mountain limestone was burnt to lime until after the Revolutionary War. The first was burned for a house built in Schuylerville. The stone was broken into small pieces and a layer of it was laid upon the top of a large log-heap which was set on fire and thus produced a sufficient heat to reduce the stone to lime. The first kiln for burning lime was built by Cornelius Dunham about sixty years ago. And one Ferrin commenced burning lime about the same time. Gardner Thayer and Samuel Heath have done more of a business at burning lime and sending it to market than anybody else in this district. The price of lime has always been two shillings per bushel here at the kilns—though sometimes in winter when the supply was limited it has been two shillings, sixpence.[104]

FIGHTING AND DRINKING

Donald McDonald:

A town meeting or other public gathering never passed, when I was a boy, without a fight. The Armstrongs were noted bullies. They were very athletic men. I remember once seeing Bob Armstrong take the "Salmon Lep"—leap like a salmon—as it was called in a barroom coming from Lansingburgh. This consisted in placing himself on the floor on all fours and then springing up and slapping his hands together three times before striking the floor again. This was a feat that few could accomplish. There was but one man in the county that could whip the Armstrongs. That was Robert Pattison. He was a large man and lived near the lime kilns in Hartford and used to burn lime there.[105]

Asa Fitch: "April 21, 1866: An old white-headed man, wandering about the country bottoming chairs, and employed today by me, tells me he is eighty-four years old. His name is Nathaniel Covill. He was born in Springfield, Vermont and came to Salem when he was a boy ten years old [1792]—working for General Williams and learning the tanner and currier's trade of Boutwell here. In 1806 he set up in the tannery business himself at Bedlam where he remained till 1816—since which he has lived around in Argyle, Greenwich,

137

etc. having no fixed residence, being apparently intemperate and spending his small earnings probably for liquor. Has four sons in the western country—two of them in the war."[106]

Nathaniel Covill:

On all public occasions, training days, court weeks, et cetera, there was all sorts of wild rude sports going on in the Village [*Salem*]—drinking and frolicking, singing songs, and always fighting was going on, wrestling and boxing, et cetera.

The town was settled with all kinds of people: Scotch, Irish, Yankee, Dutch and many Negroes. And everyone thought his own nationality the best and greatest and despised all the others, and if any remark derogatory to the Irish, the Dutch or other people was dropped in conversation, someone would instantly say, "That deserves a knock down," or words of some such purport; and throwing off their coats and rolling up their sleeves, at it they would go.

Bob Pattison was the greatest boxer and most noted bully here in those days. He did not live here [*Salem*] but was always present on public occasions, ready to whip any one that would box with him. Rowan and he were always having small fights with each other, both claiming to be the best. At length, Doctor Williams got Rowan to fight it out with Pattison and have a final end of it. A time was set for the meeting to take place back of the tan works. Pattison came punctually at the time. It was told to Rowan that Pattison was on the ground. He immediately shut up his bar and came to the spot.

His design was to run and butt his head violently into Pattison's breast or stomach and push him over, but as he came up Pattison knocked him over. At the next round, he managed to knock Pattison down. And then it was first one

138

down and then the other, without any decided advantage, till they both became so tired out they were no longer able to stand on their feet. Rowan, sitting up on the grass, sent for a bottle of liquor to give him strength to get to his house. It was a drawn game between them, neither one being the victor.

When Ladder Stewart was appointed constable, he did much towards stopping these street fights. I don't know whether his name was Robert Stewart. He was always called Ladder Stewart because at some showman's exhibition he climbed up on a ladder and looked in at a window to see the show without paying for it. He lived off south towards Sodom. Whenever a fight commenced he would command the peace and if they did not stop, he would nab them and clap them under the fish [*put them in the stocks?*]. He was so active in this that it stopped the brawls that had been so common all along till then.

After learning the tanner's trade here in Salem, I went to Albany and hired out to Hallenback, one of the principal tanners there. We had our three glasses of liquor served out to us regularly every day, morning, noon and at the close of the day, buying what more we wanted ourselves. We were paid up every Saturday and then sometimes had a "Saturday night can" to ourselves.

A fellow applied for a little job of work and did not give the customary entrance treat to the hands. A "black staff," a

139

junk bottle, was handed him but he did not fill it. We resolved to play him some trick. One trick and another was
proposed. We finally determined to get him near a watchman
and one of us throw some moosings—the fine shavings from
the rough side of hides—into the watchman's face so he would
think it was this fellow did it and would keep him overnight
in the lock-up. I prepared a pack of moosings and at the close
of the day sallied out and when he was near the watch, I
slyly came up and dashed the moosings into the watch's face
and darted out of sight around a corner. As soon as the watch
got his sight clear, seeing this fellow and knowing he came
from the tannery, he nabbed him and led him away. Next
day a policeman came to the tannery for me to go to the
police court. I was sworn. Refused to answer any question
that would criminate myself; so they got nothing out of me,
and the fellow was fined five dollars.[107]

SUPERSTITION

John Pattison:

From Eighteen Hundred and Seven till Eighteen Hundred and Fifteen, I lived at Petersburg, Rensselaer County. When residing at Petersburg, I saw a strange instance of popular superstition. The people there were Rhode Islanders and very ignorant. They had among them the belief that when a person died—at least of consumption—and another near relative was taken down with the same disease, there was some part of the deceased person remaining in the grave undecayed, deriving its sustenance from the living person who would consequently pine away and die. The only way to prevent another death in the family was to dig up the dead body, take the part which was thus living and burn it to ashes.

I went with a number of other spectators to see them dig up the body of one who, it was firmly believed, was preying upon a sick person in the same family. The grave was old and grass-grown. They came down to the coffin and raised it from the ground and opened it. There was the bones of the skeleton, the flesh all gone, its remains lying on the bottom of the coffin. In the chest was a lump of a dark color like clay, laying flattened down and decayed. No vestige of anything sound and uncorrupted could be found.

Some of the spectators jeered and laughed at the actors in this affair for their folly and they seemed to be now ashamed. The coffin was now replaced and covered up.[108]

This superstition must have been widespread. William Law of Salem gave Dr. Fitch a second-hand account of an identical incident which occurred at the Camden burying ground in Salem circa 1800.[109]

Tryphena Martin Angel:

The mare which Father brought with him from Stillwater was the first horse he ever owned. After sometime, he got well enough off to own a second horse. The horse was taken sick. What it was that ailed him nobody knew but from his actions it was concluded to be the "blind staggers." He was unable to walk straight, even, at times, to stand. At length, although he was unable to walk on the ground, he was seen to be walking up on the top of a log fence, and actually walked thus a distance of about twenty rods. This was seen by persons whose statement was credited generally. I did not see this feat myself but I saw many strange acts in the horse, and it was concluded on all hands that he was bewitched, for belief in witches was about universal at that time.[110]

Betsey Taylor:

William Tosh and his wife Jennet were from Scotland or Ireland and lived on the James Cherry Lot, Number Sixty-four, Argyle Patent. Missus Tosh was an active and very inquisitive woman—would work all night and run about all day

to gather the news. As she knew everything that was going on and would tell folks things which they had said when it was inexplicable how she had got her information, she came to be universally regarded as a witch. She was a great worker and had clothing very nice and good for one in her circumstances.

Missus Tosh was subject to bleeding at the nose. She and her husband lived alone and one night she was taken with

142

bleeding from the nose and mouth so violently that finding they could not stop it by the usual remedies, the husband ran down to Cherry's calling to Missus Cherry to make haste "for Jennie was dying." She was dead before Tosh and Missus Cherry got to the house.

Upon the same night, Alexander Livingston found a cat in his cellar lapping the cream off from the milk, as the cream had frequently been taken from the milk before. He struck the cat across the nose with a stick or club as it was running past him out of the cellar causing the blood to spurt from its nose and mouth. And it became the current report that Missus Tosh, the witch, had transformed herself into a cat and come to Livingston's cellar to lick the cream off from his milk and had thus been killed by him.

Missus Cherry [*my mother-in-law*] Missus William Taylor and a Miss Murdock dressed the body for the grave, and had a task of it, she was so large and heavy a woman. The house too was so small that they had not room to move the bed out from the wall. At length, Miss Murdock slipped her shoes off and ventured to get onto the bed behind the corpse [*to*] wash it. But she had scarcely got it raised, when the arm slid down and the cold hand of the corpse fell onto her naked foot, which so frighted her—thinking the witch was coming again to life— that at one leap she bounded to the opposite side of the room.

[*My mother-in-law*] used to relate that these notions had such an effect on her that for months afterwards when she was at the spinning wheel at night, she durst not step back to draw out the thread any farther than the length of the wheel so powerfully was it wrought into her imagination that the dead Missus Tosh was standing behind her and would catch her if she went a hair's-breadth beyond the length of the wheel. Night after night has she spun in horror from her thoughts, which she could not dispel, that this witch was behind her in the dark part of the room.[111]

NEW PIONEERS

Settlers who arrived after the Revolutionary War (and large numbers continued to come into the county up until about 1805) had an easier time than the first pioneers. Aaron Ingalsbe (b. 1765) must have come here with little or no money or supplies.

Aaron Ingalsbe:

I moved here [*Hartford*] sixty-two years ago last August in company with a party of other settlers from Worcester County, Massachuetts. Among those that came with me were my brother John, Francis Maynard, and Issacher Bates—he lived here about twenty years and then went to New Lebanon and joined the Shakers. Nine of my brothers came and settled here in town a few years after me, and my father also came and lived and died with me. When I came [*1786*], I went down to Argyle and worked for Esquire McDougall, who lived beside Scotch Lake, long enough to get a bushel of wheat and nine pounds of salted pork to live on whilst I was clearing a patch of my own land.[112]

At the time Washington County was just filling up with new settlers, some children of older residents were already heading west looking for new lands and opportunities. This letter, dated July 25, 1819 from John McCollister to his brother William in Salem, was copied by Dr. Fitch in the 1870's. It is the only written account included in this collection, and retains the author's own spelling.

John McCollister (b. 1778), his wife and six children spent the winter of 1818 in Chatauqua County. His letter describes their journey from that place to Milton, Illinois.

Sir:

We landed here the 3rd inst. (July 3) having traveled by water about 1600 miles. We started Ap 18 at the outlet of Chatauqua Lake; had rainy weather several days; saw frost the 23d for the last time but one—this was on the Allegany River two days run above Pittsburg.

April 28: Saw a man planting corn; he only furrowed the ground according to the custom of the country. This was on the Ohio at the town of Stubenville.

April 30: Apples in bloom and trees generally leaved out.

May 6: Lashed to an ark loaded with salt belonging to a Mr. Reid, a young Kentucky gentleman. After this we ran night and day when the weather was favorable.

May 10: At daylight arrived at Cincinnatti.

May 12: Arrived at the Falls of Ohio which resembled those of Stillwater. Here stands Louisville on Kentucky shore, quite a city, and Jeffersonville on Indiana side, a small thriving village. At the foot of the falls it was astonishing to see a dozen steam boats.

May 19: Mr. Reid landed at Green River, the place of his destination, and we parted with regret as his boat by running at night had helped us on very much. Our boat was so crowded as to be quite inconvenient in the daytime, being thirty-nine persons young and old to a thirty-seven feet boat eight feet wide, sloop-rigged.

May 20: Arrived at Shawneetown, the first landing place in Illinois. Here I sold my share of the boat for $50 to one of the other owners. We staid two weeks and lived in a family boat on shore that had landed in high water.

June 4: Having bought half a boat thirty-two feet long with Mr. Dunsmore from Buffalo, we started. He went by land with his family and I brought 1500 weight of freight for him which by agreement was to pay for his half—so the whole of the boat is mine. The price of the boat was $40.

June 5: Killed a deer swimming in the river.

June 7: Passed Fort Massae; called and got some milk and red cherries.

June 9: About nine we entered the noble Mississippi, and

145

to think we had now to stem the current 180 or 200 miles and that as strong as the Hudson at Lansingburgh in the highest water and much more muddy and musquatoes biting like hungrey fellows were not very pleasant feelings. I had two young men to assist, both Yorkers, one of them a sailor from Dutchess Co. But we were all unacquainted with the method of managing a boat upstream in this country. We however pushed on and by degrees learned the trade.

June 12: While lying ashore Mary fell overboard.

June 13: Rested on an island. After this, kept no record.

We passed several considerable villages before we arrived at Saint Louis, the capital of Missouri Territory. This is an elegant spot for a city and will probably soon be a large one.

July 3: Landed here it being too late to proceed on. The other boat and families had found it too late to proceed and stopped here about a week before us. They had two weeks start of us from Shawneetown.

On the whole passage we did not lose a day for rain, but we did several for head winds. Several children fell overboard coming down the Ohio River, but none of mine fell over when under way except Sanders once when he was poling up the Mississippi. Here it was necessary to keep near shore, but I had to jump in after him. And the next day I fell in myself for the first and only time. My sailor man fell over several times.

You may be surprised to hear that in this new country there are thirty or forty steamboats on the Ohio and Mississippi besides many more large keel boats; and that all the white pine boards bought at Saint Louis are brought from New York and Pennsylvania down the Ohio to the mouth, then boated up the whole distance from 15 to 1600 miles. Yet larger quantities are brought.

Saint Louis is on the Mississippi about 18 miles below the mouth of the Missouri; the mouth of the Illinois 18 above the Missouri. From where we now are we have a gentle current all the way which will be something more than 100 miles when we start again late in the fall or early in the spring. It was necessary to stop here at Wood river, a small mill stream, because it was about the last place that provisions could be bought.

I have bought a cow with a heifer calf for $22—to pay in chopping at 75 cents per cord and have almost half done. I have also taken five acres to clear and have the same price for all the cord wood and $7 per acre without fencing—a pretty good chance; and can have more if I have time to do it. I intend to pay in work, if not sick, for another cow, a yoke of oxen, and a stock of provisions before spring. You may judge by this that I have recovered of my consumptive feelings that hung around me last year. I have not been so healthy in five years as at this time, and we have had but little sickness in the family since we started in April. We have our own doctor stuff and take some now and then as a preventative.

July 26: I have this day to go to Edwardsville Land Office to get my titles recorded; ten miles from this place is the nearest post office which is the reason I have not written sooner. I can hardly spend time now to say anything about the country as my legs have got to carry me off as soon as breakfast is over. However, so far I am entirely suited with the soil and climate. I believe it will be much more healthy for me and my family than the cold regions of the north. Agues and bilious complaints are pretty common here but I am in hopes by care to avoid them.

Your affectionate brother,
John McCollister[113]

McCollister died a few weeks after he wrote this letter. He may have been stricken by one of the agues he mentions. Malarial fevers were a big problem for new settlers of wilderness areas—even in the northern states (i.e. the Genesee Fever of western New York). How sad that this hopeful, energetic man should die so suddenly. His story is a reminder of the many dangers faced by pioneer families.

McCollister's children remained to settle near Delhi and in Greene County, Illinois.

147

FOOTNOTES

1. Asa Fitch, "Notes for a History of Washington County," MSS, New York Genealogical and Biographical Society Library, Note number 161. (All future number references are to this manuscript.)
2. N.n. 849
3. N.n. 676
4. N.n. 471
5. N.n. 738
6. N.n. 46, 1060, 1065
7. N.n. 147
8. N.n. 42
9. N.n. 338
10. N.n. 997
11. N.n. 326–330
12. N.n. 997
13. N.n. 330, 331, 336
14. N.n. 150
15. N.n. 81
16. N.n. 84
17. N.n. 578
18. N.n. 1001
19. N.n. 30, 45, 92
20. N.n. 685
21. N.n. 867
22. N.n. 151
23. N.n. 176, 177
24. N.n. 927, 332
25. N.n. 339
26. N.n. 181, 182
27. N.n. 227
28. N.n. 183
29. N.n. 227
30. N.n. 193
31. N.n. 111–113
32. N.n. 471
33. N.n. 114
34. N.n. 189
35. N.n. 151
36. N.n. 115
37. N.n. 997
38. N.n. 1000
39. overleaf of N.n. 180
40. N.n. 225
41. N.n. 74
42. N.n. 853, 854, 856
43. N.n. 80
44. N.n. 82–85
45. N.n. 133, 134
46. N.n. 51
47. N.n. 88
48. N.n. 140–143
49. N.n. 51
50. N.n. 166
51. N.n. 192
52. N.n. 492
53. N.n. 229
54. N.n. 184, 683
55. N.n. 194
56. N.n. 136
57. N.n. 174, 175
58. N.n. 1062
59. Gerald Howson, *Burgoyne of Saratoga*, New York, 1979, p. 238.
60. N.n. 47, 48
61. N.n. 153–155
62. N.n. 55, 76, 193
63. N.n. 1063
64. N.n. 89
65. N.n. 156
66. N.n. 738, 742
67. N.n. 997
68. N.n. 1064
69. N.n. 116–118
70. N.n. 333
71. N.n. 498
72. N.n. 925
73. N.n. 299
74. N.n. 244
75. N.n. 122
76. N.n. 123
77. N.n. 72
78. N.n. 254–256
79. N.n. 251
80. N.n. 261, 285, 477
81. N.n. 126
82. N.n. 285
83. N.n. 261
84. N.n. 110
85. N.n. 275
86. N.n. 596
87. N.n. 274
88. N.n. 1721
89. N.n. 701
90. N.n. 315
91. N.n. 164
92. N.n. 195
93. N.n. 338
94. N.n. 226

95. N.n. 350, 351
96. N.n. 104–107
97. N.n. 847
98. N.n. 578, 581, 582
99. N.n. 315
100. N.n. 335
101. N.n. 337
102. N.n. 687, 688
103. N.n. 689
104. N.n. 248
105. N.n. 596
106. N.n. 1323
107. N.n. 1323, 1465–1468
108. N.n. 105
109. N.n. 1170
110. N.n. 870
111. N.n. 871
112. N.n. 295
113. N.n. 1889

INDEX

151

153

158

www.ingramcontent.com/pod-product-compliance
Lightning Source LLC
Chambersburg PA
CBHW061252280526
45784CB00002B/742